50 Russian Cake Recipes for Home

By: Kelly Johnson

Table of Contents

- Medovik (Honey Cake)
- Smetannik (Sour Cream Cake)
- Sharlotka (Apple Cake)
- Ptichye Moloko (Bird's Milk Cake)
- Muraveinik (Ant Hill Cake)
- Napoleon Cake
- Prague Cake
- Kartoshka (Potato Cake)
- Meringue Cake
- Cottage Cheese Cake
- Cherry Cake
- Walnut Cake
- Poppy Seed Cake
- Chocolate Cake
- Cheesecake
- Lemon Cake
- Raspberry Cake
- Strawberry Cake
- Coconut Cake
- Almond Cake
- Blueberry Cake
- Pineapple Cake
- Peach Cake
- Hazelnut Cake
- Vanilla Cake
- Marble Cake
- Caramel Cake
- Custard Cake
- Carrot Cake
- Coffee Cake
- Red Velvet Cake
- Gingerbread Cake
- Black Forest Cake
- Mocha Cake
- Chiffon Cake

- Fruitcake
- Tiramisu Cake
- Angel Food Cake
- Bundt Cake
- Lemon Poppy Seed Cake
- Spice Cake
- Rhubarb Cake
- Pistachio Cake
- Mango Cake
- Orange Cake
- Pear Cake
- Fig Cake
- Plum Cake
- Apricot Cake
- Mulberry Cake

Medovik (Honey Cake)

Ingredients:

- 3/4 cup honey
- 1 cup sugar
- 1/2 cup unsalted butter
- 3 large eggs
- 1 teaspoon baking soda
- 3 cups all-purpose flour
- 4 cups sour cream
- 1 cup powdered sugar
- 1 teaspoon vanilla extract

Instructions:

1. **Prepare the Cake Layers:**
    1. In a saucepan over medium heat, combine honey, sugar, and butter. Cook, stirring occasionally, until the sugar and butter are melted and the mixture is smooth.
    2. Remove from heat and let cool slightly.
    3. In a large bowl, whisk the eggs. Gradually add the honey mixture to the eggs, stirring constantly.
    4. Add the baking soda and mix well.
    5. Gradually add the flour, one cup at a time, mixing until a dough forms.
    6. Divide the dough into 8 equal portions. Roll each portion into a ball and flatten slightly.
2. **Bake the Cake Layers:**
    1. Preheat the oven to 350°F (175°C).
    2. Roll each portion of dough into a thin circle, about 8 inches in diameter. Use a plate or cake ring to cut out an even circle.
    3. Place each circle on a baking sheet lined with parchment paper. Bake for 5-7 minutes, or until golden brown.
    4. Remove from the oven and let cool on a wire rack.
3. **Prepare the Cream Filling:**
    1. In a large bowl, beat the sour cream, powdered sugar, and vanilla extract until smooth and well combined.
4. **Assemble the Cake:**
    1. Place one cake layer on a serving plate. Spread a generous amount of the cream filling over the layer.
    2. Repeat with the remaining layers, spreading cream filling between each layer.
    3. Spread the remaining cream filling over the top and sides of the cake.
    4. Crumble the leftover cake trimmings and sprinkle them over the top and sides of the cake for decoration.
5. **Chill and Serve:**

1. Refrigerate the assembled cake for at least 6 hours, or overnight, to allow the flavors to meld and the cake to soften.
2. Slice and serve chilled. Enjoy your Medovik!

Tips:

- The cake layers may be hard right after baking but will soften as they absorb the cream filling.
- You can add a layer of fruit preserves or jam between the cake layers for added flavor.

Smetannik (Sour Cream Cake)

Ingredients:

For the Cake:

- 2 cups all-purpose flour
- 1 teaspoon baking soda
- 1 teaspoon baking powder
- 1/2 teaspoon salt
- 1 cup granulated sugar
- 1/2 cup unsalted butter, room temperature
- 2 large eggs
- 1 cup sour cream
- 1 teaspoon vanilla extract

For the Frosting:

- 3 cups sour cream
- 1 cup powdered sugar
- 1 teaspoon vanilla extract

Instructions:

1. **Prepare the Cake:**
    1. Preheat the oven to 350°F (175°C). Grease and flour two 9-inch round cake pans.
    2. In a medium bowl, whisk together the flour, baking soda, baking powder, and salt.
    3. In a large bowl, beat the sugar and butter together until light and fluffy.
    4. Add the eggs one at a time, beating well after each addition.
    5. Mix in the sour cream and vanilla extract until well combined.
    6. Gradually add the flour mixture to the wet ingredients, mixing until just combined.
    7. Divide the batter evenly between the prepared cake pans and smooth the tops.
2. **Bake the Cake:**
    1. Bake in the preheated oven for 25-30 minutes, or until a toothpick inserted into the center comes out clean.
    2. Remove from the oven and let the cakes cool in the pans for 10 minutes.
    3. Turn the cakes out onto a wire rack to cool completely.
3. **Prepare the Frosting:**
    1. In a large bowl, beat the sour cream, powdered sugar, and vanilla extract together until smooth and well combined.
4. **Assemble the Cake:**
    1. Place one cake layer on a serving plate. Spread a generous amount of the sour cream frosting over the top.

2. Place the second cake layer on top and spread the remaining frosting over the top and sides of the cake.
5. **Chill and Serve:**
    1. Refrigerate the assembled cake for at least 2 hours, or until the frosting is set.
    2. Slice and serve chilled. Enjoy your Smetannik!

Tips:

- For added texture and flavor, you can layer fruit preserves, fresh berries, or chopped nuts between the cake layers.
- Make sure the cake layers are completely cooled before frosting to prevent the frosting from melting.
- Smetannik can be garnished with fresh fruit, nuts, or chocolate shavings for an elegant presentation.

Sharlotka (Apple Cake)

Ingredients:

- 4 large apples (Granny Smith or other tart variety)
- 3 large eggs
- 1 cup granulated sugar
- 1 cup all-purpose flour
- 1 teaspoon baking powder
- 1 teaspoon vanilla extract
- 1 teaspoon ground cinnamon (optional)
- Powdered sugar for dusting

Instructions:

1. **Prepare the Apples:**
    1. Preheat the oven to 350°F (175°C). Grease and flour a 9-inch round cake pan or springform pan.
    2. Peel, core, and slice the apples into thin wedges.
2. **Prepare the Batter:**
    1. In a large bowl, beat the eggs and sugar together until light and fluffy.
    2. Add the vanilla extract and mix well.
    3. In a separate bowl, whisk together the flour and baking powder.
    4. Gradually add the flour mixture to the egg mixture, mixing until just combined.
    5. Fold in the sliced apples. If using, add ground cinnamon to the batter and gently mix.
3. **Bake the Cake:**
    1. Pour the batter into the prepared cake pan, spreading it evenly.
    2. Bake in the preheated oven for 40-45 minutes, or until a toothpick inserted into the center comes out clean.
    3. Remove from the oven and let the cake cool in the pan for 10 minutes.
    4. Turn the cake out onto a wire rack to cool completely.
4. **Serve:**
    1. Once the cake is completely cooled, dust the top with powdered sugar.
    2. Slice and serve. Enjoy your Sharlotka!

Tips:

- For added flavor, you can add a teaspoon of lemon zest to the batter.
- Sharlotka can be served warm or at room temperature, often with a dollop of whipped cream or a scoop of vanilla ice cream.
- If you prefer a less sweet cake, you can reduce the amount of sugar slightly.

Ptichye Moloko (Bird's Milk Cake)

Ingredients:

For the Sponge Cake:

- 4 large eggs
- 1/2 cup granulated sugar
- 1/2 cup all-purpose flour
- 1/4 teaspoon baking powder

For the Soufflé:

- 1 cup milk
- 1 cup granulated sugar
- 1/4 cup cornstarch
- 1 tablespoon gelatin
- 1/4 cup cold water
- 1 cup unsalted butter, room temperature
- 1 teaspoon vanilla extract

For the Chocolate Glaze:

- 1/2 cup heavy cream
- 4 ounces dark chocolate, chopped
- 2 tablespoons unsalted butter

Instructions:

1. **Prepare the Sponge Cake:**
    1. Preheat the oven to 350°F (175°C). Grease and flour a 9-inch round cake pan.
    2. In a large bowl, beat the eggs and sugar together until light and fluffy.
    3. Sift together the flour and baking powder, then gently fold into the egg mixture until just combined.
    4. Pour the batter into the prepared cake pan and smooth the top.
    5. Bake for 20-25 minutes, or until a toothpick inserted into the center comes out clean.
    6. Remove from the oven and let the cake cool in the pan for 10 minutes. Turn out onto a wire rack to cool completely.
2. **Prepare the Soufflé:**
    1. In a small bowl, sprinkle the gelatin over the cold water and let it sit for 5-10 minutes to bloom.
    2. In a saucepan, combine the milk, sugar, and cornstarch. Cook over medium heat, stirring constantly, until the mixture thickens and comes to a boil.
    3. Remove from heat and stir in the bloomed gelatin until fully dissolved.
    4. Let the mixture cool to room temperature.

5. In a large bowl, beat the butter until light and fluffy. Gradually add the cooled milk mixture, beating until smooth and well combined.
   6. Stir in the vanilla extract.
3. **Assemble the Cake:**
   1. Place the cooled sponge cake on a serving plate.
   2. Spread the soufflé mixture evenly over the top of the sponge cake.
   3. Refrigerate the cake for at least 1 hour, or until the soufflé is set.
4. **Prepare the Chocolate Glaze:**
   1. In a small saucepan, heat the heavy cream until it just begins to simmer.
   2. Remove from heat and add the chopped dark chocolate and butter. Stir until smooth and glossy.
   3. Let the glaze cool slightly before pouring it over the chilled cake, allowing it to drip down the sides.
5. **Chill and Serve:**
   1. Refrigerate the cake for at least another hour, or until the chocolate glaze is set.
   2. Slice and serve chilled. Enjoy your Ptichye Moloko!

Tips:

- For a more decorative presentation, you can add piped whipped cream or fresh berries on top of the chocolate glaze.
- Ensure the milk mixture for the soufflé is fully cooled before adding it to the butter to prevent it from melting the butter.

Muraveinik (Ant Hill Cake)

Ingredients:

For the Dough:

- 3 cups all-purpose flour
- 1/2 cup granulated sugar
- 1 cup unsalted butter, chilled and cubed
- 1/2 cup sour cream
- 1 teaspoon baking soda
- 1 teaspoon vinegar (to activate the baking soda)
- 1 teaspoon vanilla extract

For the Cream:

- 1 can (14 oz) sweetened condensed milk
- 1 cup unsalted butter, room temperature
- 1/2 cup crushed walnuts or almonds (optional)
- 1/2 cup poppy seeds (optional)
- 1/2 cup chocolate chips (optional)

Instructions:

1. **Prepare the Dough:**
    1. In a large bowl, combine the flour and sugar.
    2. Cut the chilled butter into the flour mixture until it resembles coarse crumbs.
    3. In a small bowl, mix the baking soda and vinegar together, then add to the flour mixture.
    4. Add the sour cream and vanilla extract to the flour mixture. Mix until a dough forms.
    5. Divide the dough into 2-3 portions, wrap in plastic wrap, and refrigerate for at least 1 hour.
2. **Bake the Dough:**
    1. Preheat the oven to 350°F (175°C). Line a baking sheet with parchment paper.
    2. Grate the chilled dough using a coarse grater directly onto the prepared baking sheet.
    3. Spread the grated dough evenly and bake in the preheated oven for 20-25 minutes, or until golden brown.
    4. Remove from the oven and let cool completely.
3. **Prepare the Cream:**
    1. In a large bowl, beat the room temperature butter until light and fluffy.
    2. Gradually add the sweetened condensed milk, beating continuously until smooth and well combined.

3. If using, fold in the crushed walnuts or almonds, poppy seeds, and chocolate chips.
4. **Assemble the Cake:**
   1. Once the baked dough is completely cooled, crumble it into small pieces.
   2. In a large bowl, mix the crumbled dough with the prepared cream until the dough is well coated.
   3. Transfer the mixture to a serving plate and shape it into a mound or ant hill shape.
5. **Chill and Serve:**
   1. Refrigerate the assembled cake for at least 4 hours, or overnight, to allow the flavors to meld and the cake to set.
   2. Slice and serve chilled. Enjoy your Muraveinik!

Tips:

- You can decorate the cake with melted chocolate drizzles or sprinkle additional nuts on top for added texture and flavor.
- For a richer taste, you can use caramelized condensed milk (dulce de leche) instead of regular sweetened condensed milk.
- Make sure to chill the cake thoroughly to achieve the best texture and flavor.

Napoleon Cake

Ingredients:

For the Pastry Layers:

- 4 cups all-purpose flour
- 1 cup cold unsalted butter, cubed
- 1 cup cold water
- 1 tablespoon white vinegar
- 1/2 teaspoon salt

For the Pastry Cream:

- 4 cups whole milk
- 1 1/2 cups granulated sugar
- 4 large eggs
- 1/2 cup cornstarch
- 1/2 cup unsalted butter, room temperature
- 2 teaspoons vanilla extract

Instructions:

1. **Prepare the Pastry Dough:**
    1. In a large bowl, combine the flour and salt.
    2. Cut the cold butter into the flour mixture until it resembles coarse crumbs.
    3. In a small bowl, mix the cold water and vinegar together.
    4. Gradually add the water-vinegar mixture to the flour mixture, stirring until a dough forms.
    5. Divide the dough into 8 equal portions, shape each into a ball, wrap in plastic wrap, and refrigerate for at least 1 hour.
2. **Bake the Pastry Layers:**
    1. Preheat the oven to 400°F (200°C). Line baking sheets with parchment paper.
    2. Roll out each dough ball into a thin circle, about 9 inches in diameter. Use a plate or cake ring to trim the edges for even circles.
    3. Prick the dough circles with a fork to prevent puffing during baking.
    4. Bake each circle for 10-12 minutes, or until golden brown and crisp. Let the pastry layers cool completely.
3. **Prepare the Pastry Cream:**
    1. In a large saucepan, heat the milk until it begins to simmer.
    2. In a separate bowl, whisk together the sugar, eggs, and cornstarch until smooth.
    3. Gradually add the hot milk to the egg mixture, whisking constantly to prevent curdling.
    4. Pour the mixture back into the saucepan and cook over medium heat, stirring constantly, until thickened and boiling.

5. Remove from heat and stir in the butter and vanilla extract until smooth.
6. Let the pastry cream cool to room temperature, stirring occasionally to prevent a skin from forming.

4. **Assemble the Cake:**
    1. Place one pastry layer on a serving plate. Spread a generous amount of pastry cream over the layer.
    2. Repeat with the remaining layers, spreading pastry cream between each layer.
    3. Spread the remaining pastry cream over the top and sides of the cake.

5. **Chill and Serve:**
    1. Refrigerate the assembled cake for at least 4 hours, or overnight, to allow the flavors to meld and the layers to soften.
    2. Before serving, crush the leftover pastry trimmings and sprinkle them over the top of the cake for decoration.
    3. Slice and serve chilled. Enjoy your Napoleon Cake!

Tips:

- For a more traditional look, you can use a rolling pin to press the cake layers down gently before refrigerating to help the layers adhere better.
- The longer the cake sits, the softer and more flavorful it becomes, making it ideal to prepare a day in advance.
- If the pastry cream forms a skin while cooling, you can place a piece of plastic wrap directly on the surface to prevent this.

Prague Cake

Ingredients:

For the Chocolate Sponge Cake:

- 6 large eggs
- 1 cup granulated sugar
- 1/2 cup all-purpose flour
- 1/2 cup cocoa powder
- 1 teaspoon baking powder
- 1/4 teaspoon salt
- 1/2 cup unsalted butter, melted

For the Chocolate Cream:

- 1 cup unsalted butter, room temperature
- 1 can (14 oz) sweetened condensed milk
- 1/2 cup cocoa powder
- 1 teaspoon vanilla extract

For the Chocolate Glaze:

- 1/2 cup heavy cream
- 4 ounces dark chocolate, chopped
- 2 tablespoons unsalted butter

Instructions:

1. **Prepare the Chocolate Sponge Cake:**
    1. Preheat the oven to 350°F (175°C). Grease and line three 9-inch round cake pans with parchment paper.
    2. In a large bowl, beat the eggs and sugar together until light and fluffy.
    3. In a separate bowl, sift together the flour, cocoa powder, baking powder, and salt.
    4. Gradually fold the dry ingredients into the egg mixture until just combined.
    5. Gently fold in the melted butter.
    6. Divide the batter evenly among the prepared cake pans and smooth the tops.
    7. Bake for 20-25 minutes, or until a toothpick inserted into the center comes out clean.
    8. Remove from the oven and let the cakes cool in the pans for 10 minutes. Turn out onto a wire rack to cool completely.
2. **Prepare the Chocolate Cream:**
    1. In a large bowl, beat the butter until light and fluffy.
    2. Gradually add the sweetened condensed milk, beating continuously until smooth and well combined.

3. Add the cocoa powder and vanilla extract, and beat until the mixture is smooth and creamy.

3. **Assemble the Cake:**
    1. Place one cake layer on a serving plate. Spread a generous amount of chocolate cream over the layer.
    2. Repeat with the remaining layers, spreading chocolate cream between each layer.
    3. Spread the remaining chocolate cream over the top and sides of the cake.
4. **Prepare the Chocolate Glaze:**
    1. In a small saucepan, heat the heavy cream until it just begins to simmer.
    2. Remove from heat and add the chopped dark chocolate and butter. Stir until smooth and glossy.
    3. Let the glaze cool slightly before pouring it over the top of the cake, allowing it to drip down the sides.
5. **Chill and Serve:**
    1. Refrigerate the assembled cake for at least 2 hours, or until the chocolate glaze is set.
    2. Slice and serve chilled. Enjoy your Prague Cake!

Tips:

- For a richer flavor, you can use high-quality dark chocolate in both the cream and the glaze.
- To achieve smooth layers, you can use a serrated knife to trim the tops of the cake layers if they are uneven.
- The cake can be decorated with chocolate shavings, cocoa powder, or fresh berries for an elegant presentation.

Kartoshka (Potato Cake)

Ingredients:

- 1 pound (450g) plain vanilla or chocolate sponge cake, crumbled (store-bought or homemade)
- 1/2 cup (1 stick) unsalted butter, room temperature
- 1 can (14 oz) sweetened condensed milk
- 1/4 cup cocoa powder
- 1 teaspoon vanilla extract
- 1/2 cup chopped nuts (optional)
- Powdered sugar or cocoa powder for dusting

Instructions:

1. **Prepare the Cake Base:**
    1. Crumble the sponge cake into fine crumbs in a large bowl. You can use your hands or a food processor for this.
2. **Prepare the Cream Mixture:**
    1. In a separate bowl, beat the room temperature butter until light and fluffy.
    2. Gradually add the sweetened condensed milk, beating continuously until smooth and well combined.
    3. Add the cocoa powder and vanilla extract, and mix until the mixture is smooth and creamy.
3. **Combine Cake Crumbs and Cream:**
    1. Add the crumbled sponge cake to the cream mixture.
    2. Mix well until the crumbs are fully coated and the mixture holds together when pressed. If using, fold in the chopped nuts.
4. **Shape the Cakes:**
    1. Take small portions of the mixture and shape them into oval or potato-like shapes, about the size of a small potato.
    2. Place the shaped cakes on a parchment-lined baking sheet.
5. **Chill and Finish:**
    1. Refrigerate the cakes for at least 1 hour to firm up.
    2. Before serving, dust the cakes with powdered sugar or cocoa powder to give them a finished look.
6. **Serve:**
    1. Arrange the Kartoshka cakes on a serving platter and enjoy! These cakes are best served chilled.

Tips:

- You can add a tablespoon of rum or other liqueur to the cream mixture for an adult twist on this classic treat.
- For a richer flavor, use high-quality cocoa powder.

- Kartoshka cakes can be stored in an airtight container in the refrigerator for up to a week.

Meringue Cake

Ingredients:

For the Meringue Layers:

- 6 large egg whites, room temperature
- 1 1/2 cups granulated sugar
- 1 teaspoon vanilla extract
- 1 teaspoon white vinegar
- 1 tablespoon cornstarch

For the Cream Filling:

- 2 cups heavy cream
- 1/4 cup powdered sugar
- 1 teaspoon vanilla extract
- Fresh berries or fruit for garnish (optional)
- Mint leaves for garnish (optional)

Instructions:

1. **Prepare the Meringue Layers:**
    1. Preheat the oven to 250°F (120°C). Line two baking sheets with parchment paper. Draw three 8-inch circles on the parchment paper as guides.
    2. In a large, clean bowl, beat the egg whites until soft peaks form.
    3. Gradually add the granulated sugar, one tablespoon at a time, while continuing to beat the egg whites. Beat until the mixture is glossy and stiff peaks form.
    4. Add the vanilla extract and vinegar, and gently fold in the cornstarch until just combined.
    5. Divide the meringue mixture evenly among the three drawn circles, spreading it to fill the circles.
2. **Bake the Meringue Layers:**
    1. Bake in the preheated oven for about 1 1/2 to 2 hours, or until the meringue layers are crisp and dry. If needed, rotate the baking sheets halfway through baking to ensure even cooking.
    2. Turn off the oven and let the meringue layers cool completely in the oven with the door slightly ajar.
3. **Prepare the Cream Filling:**
    1. In a large bowl, beat the heavy cream, powdered sugar, and vanilla extract together until stiff peaks form.
4. **Assemble the Cake:**
    1. Place one meringue layer on a serving plate. Spread a third of the whipped cream over the meringue.

2. Repeat with the second meringue layer, spreading another third of the whipped cream on top.
3. Place the final meringue layer on top and spread the remaining whipped cream over the top.

5. **Garnish and Serve:**
   1. If desired, garnish the top of the cake with fresh berries, fruit, and mint leaves.
   2. Refrigerate the cake for at least 1 hour before serving to allow the layers to meld.
   3. Slice and serve chilled. Enjoy your Meringue Cake!

Tips:

- Ensure the bowl and beaters are completely clean and dry before beating the egg whites, as any fat or moisture can prevent the egg whites from whipping properly.
- Meringue cakes are best enjoyed on the day they are assembled, as the meringue can start to soften from the moisture in the cream.
- You can add a layer of lemon curd or fruit preserves between the meringue layers for added flavor and contrast.

Cottage Cheese Cake

Ingredients:

For the Crust:

- 1 1/2 cups graham cracker crumbs (about 12-14 whole crackers)
- 1/4 cup granulated sugar
- 1/2 cup unsalted butter, melted

For the Filling:

- 24 oz (about 3 cups) cottage cheese, drained well
- 1 cup granulated sugar
- 4 large eggs
- 1/4 cup all-purpose flour
- 1 teaspoon vanilla extract
- Zest of 1 lemon (optional)
- 1/2 cup sour cream (for topping)

Instructions:

1. **Prepare the Crust:**
    1. Preheat the oven to 325°F (160°C). Grease a 9-inch springform pan.
    2. In a medium bowl, mix together the graham cracker crumbs, sugar, and melted butter until well combined.
    3. Press the mixture evenly into the bottom of the prepared pan. Use the bottom of a glass or measuring cup to help compact the crust.
    4. Bake the crust in the preheated oven for 10 minutes. Remove and let cool while preparing the filling.
2. **Prepare the Filling:**
    1. In a food processor or blender, blend the cottage cheese until smooth.
    2. In a large bowl, beat together the blended cottage cheese and sugar until smooth.
    3. Add the eggs one at a time, mixing well after each addition.
    4. Mix in the flour, vanilla extract, and lemon zest (if using), until smooth and well combined.
3. **Assemble and Bake:**
    1. Pour the filling over the cooled crust in the springform pan.
    2. Tap the pan gently on the counter to remove any air bubbles.
    3. Bake in the preheated oven for 50-60 minutes, or until the center is set and the edges are lightly golden.
    4. Remove from the oven and let cool in the pan for 15-20 minutes. Then, run a knife around the edge of the pan to loosen the cake from the sides.
    5. Let the cake cool completely in the pan on a wire rack.

4. **Finish the Cake:**
    1. Once the cake has cooled, spread the sour cream evenly over the top.
    2. Refrigerate the cake for at least 4 hours, or preferably overnight, to chill and set.
    3. Before serving, carefully remove the sides of the springform pan.
    4. Slice and serve chilled. Enjoy your Cottage Cheese Cake!

Tips:

- Ensure the cottage cheese is well drained to prevent excess moisture in the filling.
- You can customize the flavor by adding raisins, dried fruit, or chocolate chips to the filling.
- Serve the cake with fresh berries or fruit compote for a delightful contrast of flavors.

Cherry Cake

Ingredients:

- 1 cup unsalted butter, softened
- 1 1/2 cups granulated sugar
- 4 large eggs
- 2 teaspoons vanilla extract
- 3 cups all-purpose flour
- 1 tablespoon baking powder
- 1/2 teaspoon salt
- 1 cup milk
- 2 cups fresh or frozen cherries, pitted and halved

For the Cherry Glaze:

- 1 cup powdered sugar
- 2-3 tablespoons cherry juice (from the cherries)
- 1/2 teaspoon almond extract (optional)

Instructions:

1. **Preheat and Prepare:**
    - Preheat your oven to 350°F (175°C). Grease and flour a 9x13-inch baking pan or two 9-inch round cake pans.
2. **Mix the Batter:**
    - In a large bowl, cream together the butter and sugar until light and fluffy.
    - Beat in the eggs one at a time, then stir in the vanilla extract.
3. **Combine Dry Ingredients:**
    - In a separate bowl, whisk together the flour, baking powder, and salt.
4. **Alternate Mixing:**
    - Gradually add the flour mixture to the creamed butter mixture, alternating with the milk. Begin and end with the flour mixture, mixing just until combined.
5. **Add Cherries:**
    - Gently fold in the cherries until evenly distributed throughout the batter.
6. **Bake:**
    - Pour the batter into the prepared baking pan(s) and spread evenly.
    - Bake in the preheated oven for 35-40 minutes (for a 9x13-inch pan) or 25-30 minutes (for round pans), or until a toothpick inserted into the center comes out clean.
7. **Make the Cherry Glaze:**
    - While the cake is baking, prepare the cherry glaze. In a small bowl, whisk together the powdered sugar, cherry juice, and almond extract (if using) until smooth. Adjust consistency with more cherry juice if needed.
8. **Glaze and Serve:**

- Once the cake is baked and cooled for about 10 minutes, drizzle the cherry glaze over the warm cake.
- Allow the cake to cool completely before slicing and serving.

Tips:

- If using frozen cherries, thaw and drain them well before using.
- You can sprinkle some sliced almonds or powdered sugar on top for added decoration.
- Serve this cake with a dollop of whipped cream or a scoop of vanilla ice cream for a delightful dessert treat!

Walnut Cake

Ingredients:

For the Cake:

- 1 cup unsalted butter, softened
- 1 cup granulated sugar
- 4 large eggs
- 2 cups all-purpose flour
- 1 teaspoon baking powder
- 1/2 teaspoon baking soda
- 1/2 teaspoon salt
- 1 cup sour cream
- 1 teaspoon vanilla extract
- 1 cup chopped walnuts

For the Frosting:

- 1/2 cup unsalted butter, softened
- 8 oz cream cheese, softened
- 4 cups powdered sugar
- 1 teaspoon vanilla extract
- Chopped walnuts for garnish (optional)

Instructions:

1. **Preheat and Prepare:**
    - Preheat your oven to 350°F (175°C). Grease and flour a 9x13-inch baking pan or two 9-inch round cake pans.
2. **Mix the Cake Batter:**
    - In a large bowl, cream together the butter and sugar until light and fluffy.
    - Add the eggs one at a time, beating well after each addition.
3. **Combine Dry Ingredients:**
    - In a separate bowl, whisk together the flour, baking powder, baking soda, and salt.
4. **Alternate Mixing:**
    - Gradually add the flour mixture to the creamed butter mixture, alternating with the sour cream. Begin and end with the flour mixture, mixing just until combined.
    - Stir in the vanilla extract and chopped walnuts.
5. **Bake:**
    - Pour the batter into the prepared baking pan(s) and spread evenly.
    - Bake in the preheated oven for 30-35 minutes (for a 9x13-inch pan) or 25-30 minutes (for round pans), or until a toothpick inserted into the center comes out clean.

- Remove from the oven and let the cake cool completely on a wire rack.

6. **Prepare the Frosting:**
   - In a medium bowl, beat together the softened butter and cream cheese until smooth and creamy.
   - Gradually add the powdered sugar, beating until light and fluffy.
   - Mix in the vanilla extract until well combined.

7. **Frost the Cake:**
   - Once the cake is completely cooled, spread the frosting evenly over the top and sides of the cake.
   - Sprinkle chopped walnuts on top for garnish, if desired.

8. **Chill and Serve:**
   - Refrigerate the cake for at least 1 hour before slicing and serving to allow the frosting to set.
   - Slice and serve chilled. Enjoy your Walnut Cake!

Tips:

- Ensure the butter and cream cheese are softened to room temperature for smooth frosting.
- You can toast the chopped walnuts lightly before adding them to the batter for a deeper nutty flavor.
- This cake pairs wonderfully with a cup of coffee or tea, or as a delightful dessert after a meal.

Poppy Seed Cake

Ingredients:

For the Cake:

- 1 cup unsalted butter, softened
- 1 1/2 cups granulated sugar
- 4 large eggs
- 1 cup sour cream
- 2 cups all-purpose flour
- 1/4 cup poppy seeds
- 1 teaspoon baking powder
- 1/2 teaspoon baking soda
- 1/2 teaspoon salt
- 1 teaspoon vanilla extract

For the Glaze:

- 1 cup powdered sugar
- 2-3 tablespoons milk
- 1/2 teaspoon vanilla extract

Instructions:

1. **Preheat and Prepare:**
    - Preheat your oven to 350°F (175°C). Grease and flour a 10-inch bundt pan or a 9x13-inch baking pan.
2. **Mix the Cake Batter:**
    - In a large bowl, cream together the softened butter and sugar until light and fluffy.
    - Add the eggs one at a time, beating well after each addition.
    - Stir in the sour cream and vanilla extract until smooth.
3. **Combine Dry Ingredients:**
    - In a separate bowl, whisk together the flour, poppy seeds, baking powder, baking soda, and salt.
4. **Mix the Batter:**
    - Gradually add the dry ingredients to the creamed mixture, mixing until just combined. Do not overmix.
5. **Bake:**
    - Pour the batter into the prepared pan and spread evenly.
    - Bake in the preheated oven for 45-50 minutes (for a bundt pan) or 30-35 minutes (for a 9x13-inch pan), or until a toothpick inserted into the center comes out clean.
    - Remove from the oven and let the cake cool in the pan for 10 minutes. Then, remove from the pan and let cool completely on a wire rack.

6. **Prepare the Glaze:**
    - In a small bowl, whisk together the powdered sugar, milk, and vanilla extract until smooth and pourable. Adjust the consistency with more milk if needed.
7. **Glaze the Cake:**
    - Once the cake is completely cooled, drizzle the glaze over the top of the cake.
    - Allow the glaze to set before slicing and serving.
8. **Serve and Enjoy:**
    - Slice and serve your delicious Poppy Seed Cake! Enjoy it with a cup of tea or coffee.

Tips:

- Make sure to properly grease and flour your baking pan to prevent the cake from sticking.
- You can add a tablespoon of lemon zest to the batter for a citrusy twist.
- Store any leftovers in an airtight container at room temperature for up to 3 days.

Chocolate Cake

Ingredients:

For the Cake:

- 1 and 3/4 cups all-purpose flour
- 1 and 1/2 teaspoons baking powder
- 1 and 1/2 teaspoons baking soda
- 1 teaspoon salt
- 1 and 3/4 cups granulated sugar
- 3/4 cup unsweetened cocoa powder
- 2 large eggs
- 1 cup whole milk
- 1/2 cup vegetable oil
- 2 teaspoons vanilla extract
- 1 cup boiling water

For the Chocolate Frosting:

- 1 cup unsalted butter, softened
- 3 and 1/2 cups powdered sugar
- 1/2 cup unsweetened cocoa powder
- 1/2 teaspoon salt
- 2 teaspoons vanilla extract
- 1/3 cup whole milk or heavy cream, more if needed

Instructions:

1. **Preheat and Prepare:**
   - Preheat your oven to 350°F (175°C). Grease and flour two 9-inch round cake pans or line them with parchment paper.
2. **Mix Dry Ingredients:**
   - In a large bowl, whisk together the flour, baking powder, baking soda, salt, granulated sugar, and cocoa powder until well combined.
3. **Add Wet Ingredients:**
   - Add the eggs, milk, vegetable oil, and vanilla extract to the dry ingredients. Beat on medium speed until well combined.
   - Reduce the mixer speed to low and carefully add the boiling water to the cake batter. Beat on high speed for about 1 minute to add air to the batter.
4. **Bake:**
   - Divide the batter evenly between the prepared cake pans.
   - Bake in the preheated oven for 30 to 35 minutes, or until a toothpick inserted into the center of the cakes comes out clean.

- Remove from the oven and allow the cakes to cool in the pans for 10 minutes before transferring them to a wire rack to cool completely.

5. **Prepare the Frosting:**
   - In a large bowl, beat the softened butter until creamy.
   - Gradually add the powdered sugar, cocoa powder, and salt, mixing until combined.
   - Add the vanilla extract and milk or cream, beating on high speed for 3-5 minutes until the frosting is light and fluffy. Add more milk or cream if needed to reach spreading consistency.

6. **Frost and Assemble:**
   - Once the cakes are completely cooled, frost the top of one cake layer with a generous amount of chocolate frosting.
   - Place the second cake layer on top and frost the entire cake with the remaining frosting.
   - You can decorate the cake with chocolate shavings, sprinkles, or berries if desired.

7. **Serve and Enjoy:**
   - Slice and serve your delicious Chocolate Cake! It's perfect for birthdays, celebrations, or simply as a delightful treat.

Tips:

- Ensure the boiling water is added carefully to the cake batter as it helps to activate the cocoa powder and create a smooth texture.
- For an extra moist cake, you can add 1/2 cup of sour cream or Greek yogurt to the batter along with the other wet ingredients.
- Store the cake covered at room temperature for up to 3 days or in the refrigerator for up to 5 days.

Cheesecake

Ingredients:

For the Crust:

- 1 and 1/2 cups graham cracker crumbs (about 12-14 whole crackers)
- 1/4 cup granulated sugar
- 1/2 cup unsalted butter, melted

For the Cheesecake Filling:

- 4 packages (8 ounces each) cream cheese, softened
- 1 and 1/4 cups granulated sugar
- 4 large eggs, room temperature
- 1 cup sour cream, room temperature
- 1/4 cup all-purpose flour
- 1 tablespoon vanilla extract
- Zest of 1 lemon (optional)

Instructions:

1. **Preheat and Prepare:**
    - Preheat your oven to 325°F (160°C). Grease a 9-inch springform pan and line the bottom with parchment paper.
2. **Make the Crust:**
    - In a medium bowl, mix together the graham cracker crumbs, sugar, and melted butter until well combined.
    - Press the mixture evenly into the bottom of the prepared springform pan.
3. **Prepare the Cheesecake Filling:**
    - In a large bowl, beat the softened cream cheese and sugar until smooth and creamy, about 2-3 minutes.
    - Add the eggs one at a time, mixing well after each addition.
    - Mix in the sour cream, flour, vanilla extract, and lemon zest (if using) until smooth and well combined. Be careful not to overmix.
4. **Bake the Cheesecake:**
    - Pour the cheesecake filling over the prepared crust in the springform pan.
    - Smooth the top with a spatula to even out the surface.
5. **Bake in Water Bath (Optional):**
    - For a creamier texture and to prevent cracking, you can place the springform pan in a larger roasting pan and fill the roasting pan with hot water halfway up the sides of the springform pan.
6. **Bake in the Oven:**
    - Bake the cheesecake in the preheated oven for 55-65 minutes, or until the edges are set and the center is slightly jiggly. The top should be lightly golden.

7. **Cool and Chill:**
    - Turn off the oven and let the cheesecake cool in the oven with the door slightly ajar for 1 hour.
    - Remove the cheesecake from the oven and let it cool completely at room temperature.
    - Once cooled, refrigerate the cheesecake for at least 4 hours, preferably overnight, to set completely.
8. **Serve:**
    - Before serving, carefully remove the sides of the springform pan.
    - Slice and serve your New York-Style Cheesecake plain or with your favorite topping, such as fresh berries, fruit compote, or chocolate sauce.

Tips:

- Ensure all ingredients are at room temperature, especially the cream cheese and eggs, to achieve a smooth and creamy cheesecake.
- Avoid overmixing the batter after adding the eggs to prevent incorporating too much air, which can lead to cracking during baking.
- For a neat slice, dip a sharp knife in hot water and wipe dry between each slice.

Enjoy your homemade New York-style cheesecake!

Lemon Cake

Ingredients:

For the Cake:

- 1 cup unsalted butter, softened
- 1 and 1/2 cups granulated sugar
- 4 large eggs, room temperature
- Zest of 2 lemons
- 3 tablespoons fresh lemon juice
- 2 and 1/2 cups all-purpose flour
- 2 teaspoons baking powder
- 1/2 teaspoon baking soda
- 1/2 teaspoon salt
- 1 cup sour cream, room temperature

For the Lemon Glaze:

- 1 cup powdered sugar
- 2-3 tablespoons fresh lemon juice
- Zest of 1 lemon (optional)

Instructions:

1. **Preheat and Prepare:**
   - Preheat your oven to 350°F (175°C). Grease and flour a 9x13-inch baking pan or two 9-inch round cake pans.
2. **Mix the Cake Batter:**
   - In a large bowl, cream together the softened butter and granulated sugar until light and fluffy.
   - Add the eggs one at a time, beating well after each addition.
   - Mix in the lemon zest and lemon juice until combined.
3. **Combine Dry Ingredients:**
   - In a separate bowl, whisk together the flour, baking powder, baking soda, and salt.
4. **Alternate Mixing:**
   - Gradually add the dry ingredients to the creamed mixture, alternating with the sour cream. Begin and end with the flour mixture, mixing just until combined.
5. **Bake:**
   - Pour the batter into the prepared pan(s) and spread evenly.
   - Bake in the preheated oven for 25-30 minutes (for round pans) or 30-35 minutes (for a 9x13-inch pan), or until a toothpick inserted into the center comes out clean.
6. **Prepare the Lemon Glaze:**

- In a small bowl, whisk together the powdered sugar and lemon juice until smooth and pourable. Adjust the consistency with more lemon juice if needed.
- Stir in the lemon zest for added flavor, if desired.

7. **Glaze the Cake:**
   - Once the cake is baked and while still warm, poke holes in the top of the cake using a skewer or fork.
   - Pour the lemon glaze over the warm cake, allowing it to soak into the cake and drizzle down the sides.

8. **Cool and Serve:**
   - Let the cake cool completely in the pan(s) on a wire rack.
   - Slice and serve your delicious Lemon Cake! It's perfect for tea time, dessert, or any special occasion.

Tips:

- For an extra lemony flavor, you can add more lemon zest to both the cake batter and the glaze.
- Make sure to use fresh lemon juice for the best flavor.
- Store any leftovers covered at room temperature for up to 3 days or in the refrigerator for up to 5 days.

Enjoy your homemade Lemon Cake!

Raspberry Cake

Ingredients:

For the Cake:

- 1 and 1/2 cups all-purpose flour
- 1 and 1/2 teaspoons baking powder
- 1/2 teaspoon baking soda
- 1/4 teaspoon salt
- 1/2 cup unsalted butter, softened
- 1 cup granulated sugar
- 2 large eggs, room temperature
- 1 teaspoon vanilla extract
- 1/2 cup sour cream
- 1/2 cup milk

For the Raspberry Filling:

- 2 cups fresh raspberries
- 1/4 cup granulated sugar
- 1 tablespoon cornstarch
- 1 tablespoon lemon juice

For the Frosting:

- 1 cup unsalted butter, softened
- 3 cups powdered sugar
- 1 teaspoon vanilla extract
- 2-3 tablespoons milk or heavy cream

Instructions:

1. **Preheat and Prepare:**
    - Preheat your oven to 350°F (175°C). Grease and flour two 9-inch round cake pans or line them with parchment paper.
2. **Make the Cake Batter:**
    - In a medium bowl, whisk together the flour, baking powder, baking soda, and salt.
    - In a large bowl, cream together the softened butter and granulated sugar until light and fluffy.
    - Add the eggs one at a time, beating well after each addition.
    - Mix in the vanilla extract.
    - Gradually add the dry ingredients to the creamed mixture, alternating with the sour cream and milk. Begin and end with the dry ingredients, mixing just until combined.
3. **Prepare the Raspberry Filling:**

- In a small saucepan, combine the raspberries, granulated sugar, cornstarch, and lemon juice.
- Cook over medium heat, stirring constantly, until the mixture thickens and comes to a boil.
- Remove from heat and let it cool completely.
4. **Assemble the Cake:**
    - Divide the cake batter evenly between the prepared cake pans.
    - Spoon the cooled raspberry filling evenly over the batter in each pan, leaving a small border around the edges.
5. **Bake:**
    - Bake in the preheated oven for 25-30 minutes, or until a toothpick inserted into the center comes out clean.
    - Remove from the oven and let the cakes cool in the pans for 10 minutes before transferring them to a wire rack to cool completely.
6. **Make the Frosting:**
    - In a large bowl, beat the softened butter until creamy.
    - Gradually add the powdered sugar, beating until smooth and fluffy.
    - Mix in the vanilla extract.
    - Add milk or cream, 1 tablespoon at a time, until the frosting reaches a spreadable consistency.
7. **Frost the Cake:**
    - Once the cakes are completely cooled, place one cake layer on a serving plate or cake stand.
    - Spread a layer of frosting over the top of the first cake layer.
    - Place the second cake layer on top and frost the entire cake with the remaining frosting.
8. **Decorate and Serve:**
    - Garnish the top of the cake with fresh raspberries, if desired.
    - Slice and serve your delicious Raspberry Cake! It's perfect for celebrations or as a special dessert treat.

Tips:

- You can use frozen raspberries for the filling if fresh ones are not available. Thaw and drain them before using.
- Ensure the raspberry filling is completely cooled before spreading it over the cake batter to prevent the layers from mixing too much.
- Store any leftovers covered in the refrigerator for up to 3 days.

Enjoy your homemade Raspberry Cake!

Strawberry Cake

Ingredients:

For the Cake:

- 1 and 1/2 cups all-purpose flour
- 1 and 1/2 teaspoons baking powder
- 1/2 teaspoon baking soda
- 1/4 teaspoon salt
- 1/2 cup unsalted butter, softened
- 1 cup granulated sugar
- 2 large eggs, room temperature
- 1 teaspoon vanilla extract
- 1/2 cup sour cream
- 1/2 cup whole milk

For the Strawberry Puree:

- 2 cups fresh strawberries, hulled and chopped
- 1/4 cup granulated sugar
- 1 tablespoon lemon juice

For the Strawberry Frosting:

- 1 cup unsalted butter, softened
- 4 cups powdered sugar
- 1/2 cup strawberry puree (strained if desired)
- 1 teaspoon vanilla extract
- Fresh strawberries for garnish (optional)

Instructions:

1. **Preheat and Prepare:**
    - Preheat your oven to 350°F (175°C). Grease and flour two 9-inch round cake pans or line them with parchment paper.
2. **Make the Cake Batter:**
    - In a medium bowl, whisk together the flour, baking powder, baking soda, and salt.
    - In a large bowl, cream together the softened butter and granulated sugar until light and fluffy.
    - Add the eggs one at a time, beating well after each addition.
    - Mix in the vanilla extract.
    - Gradually add the dry ingredients to the creamed mixture, alternating with the sour cream and milk. Begin and end with the dry ingredients, mixing just until combined.
3. **Prepare the Strawberry Puree:**

- In a blender or food processor, blend the chopped strawberries, granulated sugar, and lemon juice until smooth.
- Strain the puree through a fine mesh sieve if you prefer a smoother texture, or use as is for a more rustic texture.

4. **Bake the Cake:**
   - Divide the cake batter evenly between the prepared cake pans.
   - Bake in the preheated oven for 25-30 minutes, or until a toothpick inserted into the center comes out clean.
   - Remove from the oven and let the cakes cool in the pans for 10 minutes before transferring them to a wire rack to cool completely.

5. **Make the Strawberry Frosting:**
   - In a large bowl, beat the softened butter until creamy.
   - Gradually add the powdered sugar, mixing until smooth and fluffy.
   - Mix in the strawberry puree and vanilla extract until well combined. Adjust consistency with more powdered sugar if needed.

6. **Frost and Assemble the Cake:**
   - Place one cake layer on a serving plate or cake stand.
   - Spread a layer of strawberry frosting over the top of the first cake layer.
   - Place the second cake layer on top and frost the entire cake with the remaining strawberry frosting.

7. **Garnish and Serve:**
   - Garnish the top of the cake with fresh strawberries, sliced or whole, if desired.
   - Slice and serve your delicious Strawberry Cake! It's perfect for birthdays, parties, or any special occasion.

Tips:

- Use ripe and flavorful strawberries for the best results in both the puree and as garnish.
- Adjust the sweetness of the frosting by adding more or less powdered sugar to suit your taste.
- Store any leftovers covered in the refrigerator for up to 3 days.

Enjoy your homemade Strawberry Cake!

Coconut Cake

Ingredients:

For the Cake:

- 1 and 1/2 cups all-purpose flour
- 1 and 1/2 teaspoons baking powder
- 1/2 teaspoon baking soda
- 1/4 teaspoon salt
- 1/2 cup unsalted butter, softened
- 1 cup granulated sugar
- 2 large eggs, room temperature
- 1 teaspoon vanilla extract
- 1/2 teaspoon coconut extract (optional)
- 1/2 cup coconut milk
- 1/2 cup sour cream

For the Coconut Frosting:

- 1 cup unsalted butter, softened
- 4 cups powdered sugar
- 1/4 cup coconut milk
- 1 teaspoon vanilla extract
- 1/2 teaspoon coconut extract (optional)
- 2 cups sweetened shredded coconut, for topping

Instructions:

1. **Preheat and Prepare:**
   - Preheat your oven to 350°F (175°C). Grease and flour two 9-inch round cake pans or line them with parchment paper.
2. **Make the Cake Batter:**
   - In a medium bowl, whisk together the flour, baking powder, baking soda, and salt.
   - In a large bowl, cream together the softened butter and granulated sugar until light and fluffy.
   - Add the eggs one at a time, beating well after each addition.
   - Mix in the vanilla extract and coconut extract (if using).
   - Gradually add the dry ingredients to the creamed mixture, alternating with the coconut milk and sour cream. Begin and end with the dry ingredients, mixing just until combined.
3. **Bake the Cake:**
   - Divide the cake batter evenly between the prepared cake pans.
   - Bake in the preheated oven for 25-30 minutes, or until a toothpick inserted into the center comes out clean.

- Remove from the oven and let the cakes cool in the pans for 10 minutes before transferring them to a wire rack to cool completely.

4. **Make the Coconut Frosting:**
   - In a large bowl, beat the softened butter until creamy.
   - Gradually add the powdered sugar, mixing until smooth and fluffy.
   - Mix in the coconut milk, vanilla extract, and coconut extract (if using) until well combined and creamy.

5. **Frost and Assemble the Cake:**
   - Place one cake layer on a serving plate or cake stand.
   - Spread a layer of coconut frosting over the top of the first cake layer.
   - Place the second cake layer on top and frost the entire cake with the remaining coconut frosting.

6. **Decorate with Coconut:**
   - Press sweetened shredded coconut onto the sides and top of the frosted cake for decoration and added coconut flavor.

7. **Serve:**
   - Slice and serve your delicious Coconut Cake! It's perfect for tropical-themed parties, celebrations, or as a delightful dessert.

Tips:

- Use coconut milk for both the cake batter and frosting to enhance the coconut flavor.
- Toasted coconut can be used for garnish to add a crunchy texture and deeper coconut flavor.
- Store any leftovers covered in the refrigerator for up to 3 days.

Enjoy your homemade Coconut Cake!

Almond Cake

Ingredients:

For the Cake:

- 1 cup unsalted butter, softened
- 1 cup granulated sugar
- 4 large eggs, room temperature
- 1 teaspoon almond extract
- 1 cup all-purpose flour
- 1 cup almond flour (ground almonds)
- 1 teaspoon baking powder
- 1/4 teaspoon salt
- 1/4 cup milk

For the Almond Glaze:

- 1 cup powdered sugar
- 1-2 tablespoons milk or almond milk
- 1/2 teaspoon almond extract
- Sliced almonds, for garnish (optional)

Instructions:

1. **Preheat and Prepare:**
   - Preheat your oven to 350°F (175°C). Grease and flour a 9-inch round cake pan or line it with parchment paper.
2. **Make the Cake Batter:**
   - In a large bowl, cream together the softened butter and granulated sugar until light and fluffy.
   - Add the eggs one at a time, beating well after each addition.
   - Mix in the almond extract.
3. **Combine Dry Ingredients:**
   - In a separate bowl, whisk together the all-purpose flour, almond flour, baking powder, and salt.
4. **Mix the Batter:**
   - Gradually add the dry ingredients to the creamed mixture, alternating with the milk. Begin and end with the dry ingredients, mixing just until combined. Do not overmix.
5. **Bake the Cake:**
   - Pour the batter into the prepared cake pan and spread it evenly.
   - Bake in the preheated oven for 30-35 minutes, or until a toothpick inserted into the center comes out clean.

- Remove from the oven and let the cake cool in the pan for 10 minutes before transferring it to a wire rack to cool completely.
6. **Prepare the Almond Glaze:**
   - In a small bowl, whisk together the powdered sugar, milk or almond milk, and almond extract until smooth and pourable. Adjust the consistency with more milk if needed.
7. **Glaze the Cake:**
   - Once the cake is completely cooled, place it on a serving plate or cake stand.
   - Drizzle the almond glaze evenly over the top of the cake.
   - Garnish with sliced almonds, if desired.
8. **Serve:**
   - Slice and serve your delicious Almond Cake! It's perfect with a cup of tea or coffee, as a dessert, or for any special occasion.

Tips:

- Ensure the butter and eggs are at room temperature for smoother mixing and better texture.
- You can toast the almond flour slightly before adding it to the batter to enhance its flavor.
- Store any leftovers covered at room temperature for up to 3 days.

Enjoy your homemade Almond Cake with its delightful almond flavor!

Blueberry Cake

Ingredients:

For the Cake:

- 1 and 1/2 cups all-purpose flour
- 1 teaspoon baking powder
- 1/4 teaspoon baking soda
- 1/4 teaspoon salt
- 1/2 cup unsalted butter, softened
- 3/4 cup granulated sugar
- 2 large eggs, room temperature
- 1 teaspoon vanilla extract
- 1/2 cup sour cream
- 1/4 cup milk
- 1 and 1/2 cups fresh blueberries

For the Streusel Topping (optional):

- 1/4 cup all-purpose flour
- 1/4 cup granulated sugar
- 2 tablespoons unsalted butter, chilled and cut into small pieces

Instructions:

1. **Preheat and Prepare:**
    - Preheat your oven to 350°F (175°C). Grease and flour a 9-inch round cake pan or line it with parchment paper.
2. **Make the Streusel Topping (optional):**
    - In a small bowl, combine the flour and sugar for the streusel topping.
    - Cut in the chilled butter using a pastry cutter or fork until the mixture resembles coarse crumbs. Set aside.
3. **Prepare the Cake Batter:**
    - In a medium bowl, whisk together the flour, baking powder, baking soda, and salt.
    - In a large bowl, cream together the softened butter and granulated sugar until light and fluffy.
    - Add the eggs one at a time, beating well after each addition.
    - Mix in the vanilla extract.
    - Gradually add the dry ingredients to the creamed mixture, alternating with the sour cream and milk. Begin and end with the dry ingredients, mixing just until combined.
    - Gently fold in the fresh blueberries.
4. **Bake the Cake:**
    - Pour the batter into the prepared cake pan and spread it evenly.

- Sprinkle the streusel topping evenly over the cake batter, if using.
- Bake in the preheated oven for 30-35 minutes, or until a toothpick inserted into the center comes out clean.
- Remove from the oven and let the cake cool in the pan for 10 minutes before transferring it to a wire rack to cool completely.

5. **Serve:**
    - Slice and serve your delicious Blueberry Cake! It's perfect for brunch, dessert, or any occasion.

Tips:

- If using frozen blueberries, thaw and drain them well before folding into the batter to prevent excess moisture.
- You can dust the cooled cake with powdered sugar for an extra touch of sweetness.
- Store any leftovers covered at room temperature for up to 3 days, or in the refrigerator for longer freshness.

Enjoy your homemade Blueberry Cake with its juicy bursts of blueberries!

Pineapple Cake

Ingredients:

For the Cake:

- 2 cups all-purpose flour
- 2 teaspoons baking powder
- 1/2 teaspoon baking soda
- 1/4 teaspoon salt
- 1/2 cup unsalted butter, softened
- 1 cup granulated sugar
- 3 large eggs, room temperature
- 1 teaspoon vanilla extract
- 1 cup crushed pineapple, drained (reserve juice for syrup)
- 1/2 cup sour cream

For the Pineapple Syrup:

- 1/2 cup reserved pineapple juice
- 1/4 cup granulated sugar

For the Pineapple Cream Cheese Frosting:

- 8 ounces cream cheese, softened
- 1/2 cup unsalted butter, softened
- 4 cups powdered sugar
- 1 teaspoon vanilla extract
- 1/2 cup crushed pineapple, drained and squeezed dry

Instructions:

1. **Preheat and Prepare:**
    - Preheat your oven to 350°F (175°C). Grease and flour two 9-inch round cake pans or line them with parchment paper.
2. **Make the Cake Batter:**
    - In a medium bowl, whisk together the flour, baking powder, baking soda, and salt.
    - In a large bowl, cream together the softened butter and granulated sugar until light and fluffy.
    - Add the eggs one at a time, beating well after each addition.
    - Mix in the vanilla extract.
    - Gradually add the dry ingredients to the creamed mixture, alternating with the sour cream. Begin and end with the dry ingredients, mixing just until combined.
    - Fold in the crushed pineapple until evenly distributed.
3. **Bake the Cake:**
    - Divide the batter evenly between the prepared cake pans.

- Bake in the preheated oven for 25-30 minutes, or until a toothpick inserted into the center comes out clean.
- Remove from the oven and let the cakes cool in the pans for 10 minutes before transferring them to a wire rack to cool completely.

4. **Make the Pineapple Syrup:**
   - In a small saucepan, combine the reserved pineapple juice and granulated sugar.
   - Heat over medium heat, stirring occasionally, until the sugar is dissolved and the mixture is slightly thickened.
   - Remove from heat and let it cool.

5. **Prepare the Pineapple Cream Cheese Frosting:**
   - In a large bowl, beat together the softened cream cheese and butter until smooth and creamy.
   - Gradually add the powdered sugar, mixing until smooth and fluffy.
   - Mix in the vanilla extract.
   - Fold in the drained and squeezed dry crushed pineapple until evenly distributed.

6. **Assemble the Cake:**
   - Place one cake layer on a serving plate or cake stand.
   - Brush the top with some of the cooled pineapple syrup.
   - Spread a layer of pineapple cream cheese frosting over the top.
   - Place the second cake layer on top and brush with the remaining pineapple syrup.
   - Frost the entire cake with the remaining pineapple cream cheese frosting.

7. **Decorate and Serve:**
   - Garnish with additional crushed pineapple or toasted coconut, if desired.
   - Slice and serve your delicious Pineapple Cake! It's perfect for summer gatherings, birthdays, or any tropical-themed occasion.

Tips:

- Ensure the crushed pineapple is well drained and squeezed dry to avoid adding excess moisture to the cake batter and frosting.
- For a smoother frosting, you can strain the crushed pineapple after draining to remove excess juices.
- Store any leftovers covered in the refrigerator for up to 3 days.

Enjoy your homemade Pineapple Cake with its tropical flavors and creamy frosting!

Peach Cake

Ingredients:

For the Cake:

- 2 cups all-purpose flour
- 2 teaspoons baking powder
- 1/2 teaspoon baking soda
- 1/4 teaspoon salt
- 1/2 cup unsalted butter, softened
- 1 cup granulated sugar
- 2 large eggs, room temperature
- 1 teaspoon vanilla extract
- 1/2 cup sour cream
- 1/2 cup milk
- 2 cups fresh peaches, peeled and diced (about 2-3 medium peaches)

For the Peach Glaze:

- 1 cup powdered sugar
- 2-3 tablespoons peach juice (reserved from peeling and dicing peaches)
- 1/2 teaspoon vanilla extract

Instructions:

1. **Preheat and Prepare:**
    - Preheat your oven to 350°F (175°C). Grease and flour a 9x13-inch baking pan or two 9-inch round cake pans, or line them with parchment paper.
2. **Make the Cake Batter:**
    - In a medium bowl, whisk together the flour, baking powder, baking soda, and salt.
    - In a large bowl, cream together the softened butter and granulated sugar until light and fluffy.
    - Add the eggs one at a time, beating well after each addition.
    - Mix in the vanilla extract.
    - Gradually add the dry ingredients to the creamed mixture, alternating with the sour cream and milk. Begin and end with the dry ingredients, mixing just until combined.
    - Gently fold in the diced peaches.
3. **Bake the Cake:**
    - Pour the batter into the prepared baking pan(s) and spread it evenly.
    - Bake in the preheated oven for 30-35 minutes (for a 9x13-inch pan) or 25-30 minutes (for round pans), or until a toothpick inserted into the center comes out clean.

- Remove from the oven and let the cake cool in the pan(s) for 10 minutes before transferring it to a wire rack to cool completely.

4. **Make the Peach Glaze:**
   - In a small bowl, whisk together the powdered sugar, peach juice, and vanilla extract until smooth and pourable. Adjust the consistency with more peach juice or powdered sugar as needed.

5. **Glaze the Cake:**
   - Once the cake is completely cooled, drizzle the peach glaze evenly over the top.
   - Allow the glaze to set for a few minutes before slicing and serving.

6. **Serve:**
   - Slice and serve your delicious Peach Cake! It's perfect for summer gatherings, brunch, or as a delightful dessert.

Tips:

- Use ripe, fresh peaches for the best flavor. You can also use canned peaches (drained well) if fresh ones aren't available.
- If you prefer a more intense peach flavor, you can add a tablespoon of peach schnapps or peach liqueur to the glaze.
- Store any leftovers covered at room temperature for up to 3 days.

Enjoy your homemade Peach Cake with its juicy peach pieces and sweet glaze!

Hazelnut Cake

Ingredients:

For the Cake:

- 1 cup hazelnuts, toasted and finely ground
- 1 cup all-purpose flour
- 1 and 1/2 teaspoons baking powder
- 1/2 teaspoon baking soda
- 1/4 teaspoon salt
- 1/2 cup unsalted butter, softened
- 1 cup granulated sugar
- 3 large eggs, room temperature
- 1 teaspoon vanilla extract
- 1/2 cup sour cream
- 1/2 cup milk

For the Hazelnut Buttercream Frosting:

- 1 cup unsalted butter, softened
- 3 cups powdered sugar
- 1/2 cup hazelnut spread (such as Nutella)
- 1 teaspoon vanilla extract
- 2-3 tablespoons milk or cream, as needed

Instructions:

1. **Preheat and Prepare:**
    - Preheat your oven to 350°F (175°C). Grease and flour two 9-inch round cake pans or line them with parchment paper.
2. **Prepare Hazelnuts:**
    - Toast the hazelnuts in a dry skillet over medium heat until fragrant and lightly browned. Allow them to cool, then finely grind them in a food processor or blender.
3. **Make the Cake Batter:**
    - In a medium bowl, whisk together the ground hazelnuts, flour, baking powder, baking soda, and salt.
    - In a large bowl, cream together the softened butter and granulated sugar until light and fluffy.
    - Add the eggs one at a time, beating well after each addition.
    - Mix in the vanilla extract.
    - Gradually add the dry ingredients to the creamed mixture, alternating with the sour cream and milk. Begin and end with the dry ingredients, mixing just until combined.

4. **Bake the Cake:**
   - Divide the batter evenly between the prepared cake pans.
   - Bake in the preheated oven for 25-30 minutes, or until a toothpick inserted into the center comes out clean.
   - Remove from the oven and let the cakes cool in the pans for 10 minutes before transferring them to a wire rack to cool completely.
5. **Make the Hazelnut Buttercream Frosting:**
   - In a large bowl, beat the softened butter until creamy.
   - Gradually add the powdered sugar, mixing until smooth and fluffy.
   - Mix in the hazelnut spread and vanilla extract until well combined.
   - Add milk or cream, 1 tablespoon at a time, until the frosting reaches a spreadable consistency.
6. **Frost and Assemble the Cake:**
   - Place one cake layer on a serving plate or cake stand.
   - Spread a layer of hazelnut buttercream frosting over the top.
   - Place the second cake layer on top and frost the entire cake with the remaining hazelnut buttercream frosting.
7. **Decorate (optional):**
   - Garnish with chopped hazelnuts or chocolate shavings for extra flavor and decoration.
8. **Serve:**
   - Slice and serve your delicious Hazelnut Cake! It's perfect for special occasions or as a decadent dessert treat.

Tips:

- Ensure the hazelnuts are finely ground for a smooth texture in the cake.
- Adjust the sweetness of the frosting by adding more or less powdered sugar to suit your taste.
- Store any leftovers covered in the refrigerator for up to 3 days.

Enjoy your homemade Hazelnut Cake with its nutty flavor and creamy frosting!

Vanilla Cake

Ingredients:

For the Cake:

- 2 and 1/2 cups all-purpose flour
- 2 teaspoons baking powder
- 1/2 teaspoon baking soda
- 1/2 teaspoon salt
- 1 cup unsalted butter, softened
- 1 and 3/4 cups granulated sugar
- 4 large eggs, room temperature
- 1 tablespoon vanilla extract
- 1 cup buttermilk

For the Vanilla Buttercream Frosting:

- 1 cup unsalted butter, softened
- 4 cups powdered sugar
- 2 teaspoons vanilla extract
- 2-4 tablespoons heavy cream or milk
- Pinch of salt (optional)

Instructions:

1. **Preheat and Prepare:**
    - Preheat your oven to 350°F (175°C). Grease and flour three 8-inch round cake pans, or line them with parchment paper.
2. **Make the Cake Batter:**
    - In a medium bowl, whisk together the flour, baking powder, baking soda, and salt.
    - In a large bowl, cream together the softened butter and granulated sugar until light and fluffy.
    - Add the eggs one at a time, beating well after each addition.
    - Mix in the vanilla extract.
    - Gradually add the dry ingredients to the creamed mixture, alternating with the buttermilk. Begin and end with the dry ingredients, mixing just until combined.
3. **Bake the Cake:**
    - Divide the batter evenly between the prepared cake pans.
    - Bake in the preheated oven for 25-30 minutes, or until a toothpick inserted into the center comes out clean.
    - Remove from the oven and let the cakes cool in the pans for 10 minutes before transferring them to a wire rack to cool completely.
4. **Make the Vanilla Buttercream Frosting:**
    - In a large bowl, beat the softened butter until creamy.

- Gradually add the powdered sugar, mixing until smooth and fluffy.
- Mix in the vanilla extract and salt (if using).
- Add heavy cream or milk, 1 tablespoon at a time, until the frosting reaches a spreadable consistency.

5. **Frost and Assemble the Cake:**
    - Place one cake layer on a serving plate or cake stand.
    - Spread a layer of vanilla buttercream frosting over the top.
    - Repeat with the remaining cake layers, stacking them on top of each other and frosting between each layer.
    - Frost the top and sides of the cake with the remaining vanilla buttercream frosting.
6. **Decorate (optional):**
    - You can decorate the cake with sprinkles, edible flowers, or any other decorations of your choice.
7. **Serve:**
    - Slice and serve your delicious Vanilla Cake! It's perfect for birthdays, celebrations, or as a simple yet elegant dessert.

Tips:

- Ensure all ingredients are at room temperature for smoother mixing and better texture.
- For a lighter frosting, whip the butter for a few minutes before adding the powdered sugar.
- Store any leftovers covered in the refrigerator for up to 3 days.

Enjoy your homemade Vanilla Cake with its classic flavor and creamy frosting!

Marble Cake

Ingredients:

For the Vanilla Cake Batter:

- 1 and 3/4 cups all-purpose flour
- 1 and 1/2 teaspoons baking powder
- 1/2 teaspoon baking soda
- 1/4 teaspoon salt
- 1/2 cup unsalted butter, softened
- 1 cup granulated sugar
- 2 large eggs, room temperature
- 1 teaspoon vanilla extract
- 1/2 cup sour cream
- 1/2 cup milk

For the Chocolate Cake Batter:

- 1/4 cup unsweetened cocoa powder
- 2 tablespoons hot water

For the Chocolate Swirl:

- 1/2 cup chocolate chips or chopped chocolate
- 2 tablespoons unsalted butter

Instructions:

1. **Preheat and Prepare:**
    - Preheat your oven to 350°F (175°C). Grease and flour a 9x5-inch loaf pan or line it with parchment paper.
2. **Make the Vanilla Cake Batter:**
    - In a medium bowl, whisk together the flour, baking powder, baking soda, and salt.
    - In a large bowl, cream together the softened butter and granulated sugar until light and fluffy.
    - Add the eggs one at a time, beating well after each addition.
    - Mix in the vanilla extract.
    - Gradually add the dry ingredients to the creamed mixture, alternating with the sour cream and milk. Begin and end with the dry ingredients, mixing just until combined. Set aside.
3. **Make the Chocolate Cake Batter:**
    - In a small bowl, dissolve the cocoa powder in hot water until smooth. Let it cool slightly.
4. **Create the Chocolate Swirl:**

- In a microwave-safe bowl, melt the chocolate chips and butter in short intervals, stirring between each, until smooth and melted. Let it cool slightly.

5. **Combine Batters and Swirl:**
    - Pour half of the vanilla cake batter into the prepared loaf pan.
    - Stir the cocoa mixture into the remaining vanilla batter until well combined, creating the chocolate cake batter.
    - Drop spoonfuls of the chocolate batter over the vanilla batter in the pan.
    - Pour the melted chocolate swirl over the batter in the pan.
    - Use a knife or skewer to gently swirl the batters together, creating a marbled effect. Be careful not to overmix.

6. **Bake the Cake:**
    - Bake in the preheated oven for 50-60 minutes, or until a toothpick inserted into the center comes out clean.
    - Remove from the oven and let the cake cool in the pan for 10-15 minutes before transferring it to a wire rack to cool completely.

7. **Serve:**
    - Slice and serve your delicious Marble Cake! It's perfect for afternoon tea, dessert, or any special occasion.

Tips:

- Ensure the chocolate swirl mixture is still pourable but slightly cooled before adding to the cake batter.
- You can adjust the intensity of the chocolate flavor by adding more or less cocoa powder to the chocolate batter.
- Store any leftovers covered at room temperature for up to 3 days.

Enjoy your homemade Marble Cake with its beautiful swirls of vanilla and chocolate!

Caramel Cake

Ingredients:

For the Cake:

- 2 cups all-purpose flour
- 1 and 1/2 teaspoons baking powder
- 1/2 teaspoon baking soda
- 1/4 teaspoon salt
- 1 cup unsalted butter, softened
- 1 cup granulated sugar
- 1 cup brown sugar, packed
- 4 large eggs, room temperature
- 1 tablespoon vanilla extract
- 1 cup buttermilk

For the Caramel Sauce:

- 1 cup granulated sugar
- 6 tablespoons unsalted butter, cut into pieces
- 1/2 cup heavy cream
- Pinch of salt

For the Caramel Frosting:

- 1 cup unsalted butter, softened
- 1 cup caramel sauce (from above), cooled to room temperature
- 4 cups powdered sugar
- 1 teaspoon vanilla extract
- Pinch of salt, to taste

Instructions:

1. **Preheat and Prepare:**
   - Preheat your oven to 350°F (175°C). Grease and flour three 8-inch round cake pans, or line them with parchment paper.
2. **Make the Cake Batter:**
   - In a medium bowl, whisk together the flour, baking powder, baking soda, and salt.
   - In a large bowl, cream together the softened butter, granulated sugar, and brown sugar until light and fluffy.
   - Add the eggs one at a time, beating well after each addition.
   - Mix in the vanilla extract.
   - Gradually add the dry ingredients to the creamed mixture, alternating with the buttermilk. Begin and end with the dry ingredients, mixing just until combined.
3. **Bake the Cake:**

- Divide the batter evenly between the prepared cake pans.
- Bake in the preheated oven for 25-30 minutes, or until a toothpick inserted into the center comes out clean.
- Remove from the oven and let the cakes cool in the pans for 10 minutes before transferring them to a wire rack to cool completely.

4. **Make the Caramel Sauce:**
   - In a medium saucepan, heat the granulated sugar over medium heat, stirring constantly with a heat-resistant spatula or wooden spoon.
   - As the sugar melts, it will clump together, then eventually turn into a smooth amber-colored liquid.
   - Once the sugar is completely melted and amber in color, add the butter. Be careful as it may bubble up.
   - Stir until the butter is melted and well combined with the caramel.
   - Slowly drizzle in the heavy cream while stirring constantly. The mixture will bubble again.
   - Cook for another minute, then remove from heat and stir in a pinch of salt.
   - Let the caramel sauce cool to room temperature.

5. **Make the Caramel Frosting:**
   - In a large bowl, beat the softened butter until creamy.
   - Gradually add the powdered sugar, mixing until smooth and fluffy.
   - Mix in 1 cup of cooled caramel sauce (reserve the remaining sauce for drizzling over the cake).
   - Add vanilla extract and a pinch of salt, adjusting to taste.

6. **Frost and Assemble the Cake:**
   - Place one cake layer on a serving plate or cake stand.
   - Spread a layer of caramel frosting over the top.
   - Repeat with the remaining cake layers, stacking them on top of each other and frosting between each layer.
   - Frost the top and sides of the cake with the remaining caramel frosting.

7. **Decorate (optional):**
   - Drizzle the remaining caramel sauce over the top of the cake for a beautiful finish.
   - You can garnish with chopped nuts or a sprinkle of sea salt if desired.

8. **Serve:**
   - Slice and serve your decadent Caramel Cake! It's perfect for celebrations, parties, or whenever you crave something sweet and indulgent.

Tips:

- Ensure the caramel sauce is completely cooled before adding it to the frosting to avoid melting the butter.
- Store any leftovers covered in the refrigerator for up to 3 days.

Enjoy your homemade Caramel Cake with its rich caramel flavor and creamy frosting!

Custard Cake

Ingredients:

For the Cake:

- 1 cup all-purpose flour
- 1 teaspoon baking powder
- 1/4 teaspoon salt
- 1/2 cup unsalted butter, softened
- 1/2 cup granulated sugar
- 2 large eggs, room temperature
- 1 teaspoon vanilla extract
- 1/4 cup milk

For the Custard Layer:

- 2 cups whole milk
- 1/2 cup granulated sugar
- 1/2 cup all-purpose flour
- 4 large egg yolks
- 1 teaspoon vanilla extract

Instructions:

1. **Preheat and Prepare:**
    - Preheat your oven to 350°F (175°C). Grease and flour an 8-inch square baking dish or line it with parchment paper.
2. **Make the Cake Batter:**
    - In a medium bowl, whisk together the flour, baking powder, and salt.
    - In a separate large bowl, cream together the softened butter and granulated sugar until light and fluffy.
    - Add the eggs one at a time, beating well after each addition.
    - Mix in the vanilla extract.
    - Gradually add the dry ingredients to the creamed mixture, alternating with the milk. Begin and end with the dry ingredients, mixing just until combined.
    - Spread the cake batter evenly into the prepared baking dish.
3. **Prepare the Custard Layer:**
    - In a saucepan, heat the whole milk until steaming but not boiling.
    - In a medium bowl, whisk together the sugar and flour.
    - Whisk in the egg yolks until smooth.
    - Gradually whisk the hot milk into the egg mixture, a little at a time, to temper the eggs.
    - Pour the mixture back into the saucepan and cook over medium heat, whisking constantly, until thickened to a custard consistency (about 5-7 minutes).

- Remove from heat and stir in the vanilla extract.
4. **Assemble and Bake:**
    - Carefully pour the custard mixture over the cake batter in the baking dish. It will sink slightly into the batter.
    - Bake in the preheated oven for 40-45 minutes, or until the custard is set and the top is golden brown.
    - Remove from the oven and let the cake cool completely in the baking dish on a wire rack.
5. **Serve:**
    - Once cooled, slice and serve your delicious Custard Cake! It can be enjoyed warm or chilled.

Tips:

- Make sure to whisk the custard constantly while cooking to prevent lumps and ensure a smooth texture.
- You can dust the top with powdered sugar or serve with fresh berries for a delightful presentation.
- Store any leftovers covered in the refrigerator for up to 3 days.

Enjoy your homemade Custard Cake with its comforting combination of cake and creamy custard!

Carrot Cake

Ingredients:

For the Cake:

- 2 cups all-purpose flour
- 2 teaspoons baking powder
- 1 and 1/2 teaspoons baking soda
- 1/2 teaspoon salt
- 1 teaspoon ground cinnamon
- 1/2 teaspoon ground nutmeg
- 1/2 teaspoon ground ginger
- 1 cup granulated sugar
- 1 cup brown sugar, packed
- 1 cup vegetable oil
- 4 large eggs, room temperature
- 1 teaspoon vanilla extract
- 3 cups grated carrots (about 4-5 medium carrots)
- 1 cup crushed pineapple, drained (optional)
- 1 cup chopped walnuts or pecans (optional)

For the Cream Cheese Frosting:

- 1/2 cup unsalted butter, softened
- 8 oz cream cheese, softened
- 4 cups powdered sugar, sifted
- 1 teaspoon vanilla extract

Instructions:

1. **Preheat and Prepare:**
   - Preheat your oven to 350°F (175°C). Grease and flour three 8-inch round cake pans, or line them with parchment paper.
2. **Make the Cake Batter:**
   - In a medium bowl, whisk together the flour, baking powder, baking soda, salt, cinnamon, nutmeg, and ginger.
   - In a large bowl, whisk together the granulated sugar, brown sugar, and vegetable oil until well combined.
   - Add the eggs one at a time, beating well after each addition.
   - Stir in the vanilla extract.
   - Gradually add the dry ingredients to the wet ingredients, mixing until just combined.
   - Fold in the grated carrots, crushed pineapple (if using), and chopped nuts (if using) until evenly distributed.

3. **Bake the Cake:**
   - Divide the batter evenly between the prepared cake pans.
   - Bake in the preheated oven for 25-30 minutes, or until a toothpick inserted into the center comes out clean.
   - Remove from the oven and let the cakes cool in the pans for 10 minutes before transferring them to a wire rack to cool completely.
4. **Make the Cream Cheese Frosting:**
   - In a large bowl, beat the softened butter and cream cheese together until smooth and creamy.
   - Gradually add the powdered sugar, one cup at a time, beating well after each addition.
   - Mix in the vanilla extract until smooth and fluffy.
5. **Frost and Assemble the Cake:**
   - Place one cake layer on a serving plate or cake stand.
   - Spread a layer of cream cheese frosting over the top.
   - Repeat with the remaining cake layers, stacking them on top of each other and frosting between each layer.
   - Frost the top and sides of the cake with the remaining cream cheese frosting.
6. **Decorate (optional):**
   - Optionally, garnish with additional chopped nuts or grated carrots on top.
7. **Serve:**
   - Slice and serve your delicious Carrot Cake! It's perfect for birthdays, celebrations, or as a comforting dessert.

Tips:

- Ensure the cream cheese and butter are both softened to room temperature for a smooth and creamy frosting.
- For extra flavor, you can add a pinch of ground cloves or allspice to the cake batter.
- Store any leftovers covered in the refrigerator for up to 5 days.

Enjoy your homemade Carrot Cake with its moist texture, rich spices, and creamy frosting!

Coffee Cake

Ingredients:

For the Cake:

- 2 cups all-purpose flour
- 1 teaspoon baking powder
- 1/2 teaspoon baking soda
- 1/2 teaspoon salt
- 1/2 cup unsalted butter, softened
- 1 cup granulated sugar
- 2 large eggs, room temperature
- 1 cup sour cream or plain Greek yogurt
- 1 teaspoon vanilla extract

For the Streusel Topping:

- 1/2 cup packed brown sugar
- 1/2 cup all-purpose flour
- 1 teaspoon ground cinnamon
- 1/4 cup unsalted butter, melted

For the Glaze (optional):

- 1/2 cup powdered sugar
- 1-2 tablespoons milk or cream
- 1/2 teaspoon vanilla extract

Instructions:

1. **Preheat and Prepare:**
    - Preheat your oven to 350°F (175°C). Grease and flour a 9x9-inch square baking dish or line it with parchment paper.
2. **Make the Streusel Topping:**
    - In a medium bowl, combine the brown sugar, flour, and ground cinnamon.
    - Stir in the melted butter until the mixture resembles coarse crumbs. Set aside.
3. **Make the Cake Batter:**
    - In a medium bowl, whisk together the flour, baking powder, baking soda, and salt.
    - In a large bowl, cream together the softened butter and granulated sugar until light and fluffy.
    - Add the eggs one at a time, beating well after each addition.
    - Mix in the sour cream (or Greek yogurt) and vanilla extract until well combined.
    - Gradually add the dry ingredients to the wet ingredients, mixing until just combined. Do not overmix.
4. **Assemble and Bake:**

- Spread half of the cake batter into the prepared baking dish.
- Sprinkle half of the streusel topping evenly over the batter.
- Spread the remaining cake batter over the streusel layer.
- Top with the remaining streusel topping, spreading it evenly.

5. **Bake the Cake:**
   - Bake in the preheated oven for 35-40 minutes, or until a toothpick inserted into the center comes out clean.
   - Remove from the oven and let the cake cool in the baking dish on a wire rack.
6. **Make the Glaze (optional):**
   - In a small bowl, whisk together the powdered sugar, milk or cream, and vanilla extract until smooth.
   - Drizzle the glaze over the cooled Coffee Cake before serving.
7. **Serve:**
   - Slice and serve your delicious Coffee Cake warm or at room temperature.

Tips:

- You can add chopped nuts or dried fruits to the streusel topping for extra flavor and texture.
- Store any leftovers covered at room temperature for up to 3 days.

Enjoy your homemade Coffee Cake with its tender crumb and irresistible cinnamon streusel topping!

Red Velvet Cake

Ingredients:

For the Cake:

- 2 and 1/2 cups all-purpose flour
- 1 and 1/2 cups granulated sugar
- 1 teaspoon baking soda
- 1 teaspoon salt
- 1 teaspoon cocoa powder
- 1 and 1/2 cups vegetable oil
- 1 cup buttermilk, room temperature
- 2 large eggs, room temperature
- 2 tablespoons red food coloring
- 1 teaspoon vanilla extract
- 1 teaspoon white vinegar

For the Cream Cheese Frosting:

- 16 oz (2 packages) cream cheese, softened
- 1/2 cup unsalted butter, softened
- 4 cups powdered sugar, sifted
- 1 teaspoon vanilla extract

Instructions:

1. **Preheat and Prepare:**
   - Preheat your oven to 350°F (175°C). Grease and flour three 8-inch round cake pans, or line them with parchment paper.
2. **Make the Cake Batter:**
   - In a large bowl, sift together the flour, sugar, baking soda, salt, and cocoa powder.
   - In another bowl, whisk together the vegetable oil, buttermilk, eggs, red food coloring, vanilla extract, and white vinegar until well combined.
   - Gradually add the wet ingredients to the dry ingredients, mixing until just combined and smooth. Do not overmix.
   - Divide the batter evenly between the prepared cake pans.
3. **Bake the Cake:**
   - Bake in the preheated oven for 25-30 minutes, or until a toothpick inserted into the center comes out clean.
   - Remove from the oven and let the cakes cool in the pans for 10 minutes before transferring them to a wire rack to cool completely.
4. **Make the Cream Cheese Frosting:**

- In a large bowl, beat the softened cream cheese and butter together until smooth and creamy.
- Gradually add the powdered sugar, one cup at a time, beating well after each addition.
- Mix in the vanilla extract until smooth and fluffy.

5. **Frost and Assemble the Cake:**
    - Place one cake layer on a serving plate or cake stand.
    - Spread a layer of cream cheese frosting over the top.
    - Repeat with the remaining cake layers, stacking them on top of each other and frosting between each layer.
    - Frost the top and sides of the cake with the remaining cream cheese frosting.
6. **Decorate (optional):**
    - You can decorate the cake with red velvet cake crumbs, chocolate shavings, or fresh berries.
7. **Serve:**
    - Slice and serve your delicious Red Velvet Cake! It's perfect for birthdays, holidays, or any special occasion.

Tips:

- Ensure the cream cheese and butter are both softened to room temperature for a smooth and creamy frosting.
- If you prefer a deeper red color, you can adjust the amount of red food coloring.
- Store any leftovers covered in the refrigerator for up to 5 days.

Enjoy your homemade Red Velvet Cake with its velvety texture and creamy frosting!

Gingerbread Cake

Ingredients:

For the Cake:

- 2 and 1/2 cups all-purpose flour
- 1 and 1/2 teaspoons baking soda
- 1 teaspoon baking powder
- 1/2 teaspoon salt
- 2 teaspoons ground ginger
- 1 and 1/2 teaspoons ground cinnamon
- 1/4 teaspoon ground cloves
- 1/4 teaspoon ground nutmeg
- 1/2 cup unsalted butter, softened
- 1/2 cup granulated sugar
- 1/2 cup brown sugar, packed
- 2 large eggs, room temperature
- 1 cup unsulphured molasses
- 1 cup hot water

For the Cream Cheese Frosting:

- 8 oz cream cheese, softened
- 1/4 cup unsalted butter, softened
- 2 cups powdered sugar, sifted
- 1 teaspoon vanilla extract

Instructions:

1. **Preheat and Prepare:**
    - Preheat your oven to 350°F (175°C). Grease and flour a 9x13-inch baking dish, or line it with parchment paper.
2. **Make the Cake Batter:**
    - In a medium bowl, whisk together the flour, baking soda, baking powder, salt, ground ginger, cinnamon, cloves, and nutmeg.
    - In a large bowl, cream together the softened butter, granulated sugar, and brown sugar until light and fluffy.
    - Add the eggs one at a time, beating well after each addition.
    - Mix in the molasses until well combined.
    - Gradually add the dry ingredients to the wet ingredients, alternating with the hot water. Begin and end with the dry ingredients, mixing until just combined.
3. **Bake the Cake:**
    - Pour the batter into the prepared baking dish, spreading it evenly.

- Bake in the preheated oven for 30-35 minutes, or until a toothpick inserted into the center comes out clean.
- Remove from the oven and let the cake cool completely in the baking dish on a wire rack.

4. **Make the Cream Cheese Frosting:**
   - In a large bowl, beat the softened cream cheese and butter together until smooth and creamy.
   - Gradually add the powdered sugar, one cup at a time, beating well after each addition.
   - Mix in the vanilla extract until smooth and fluffy.

5. **Frost the Cake:**
   - Once the cake has cooled completely, spread the cream cheese frosting evenly over the top.
   - Optionally, sprinkle with a little ground cinnamon or decorate with gingerbread cookie crumbs for an extra festive touch.

6. **Serve:**
   - Slice and serve your delicious Gingerbread Cake! It's wonderful served warm or at room temperature.

Tips:

- For a richer flavor, you can add 1/2 cup chopped crystallized ginger to the cake batter.
- Store any leftovers covered in the refrigerator for up to 5 days.

Enjoy the warm spices and rich flavors of your homemade Gingerbread Cake, perfect for holiday gatherings or cozy winter evenings!

Black Forest Cake

Ingredients:

For the Chocolate Sponge Cake:

- 1 and 1/2 cups all-purpose flour
- 1 and 1/2 cups granulated sugar
- 1/2 cup unsweetened cocoa powder
- 1 and 1/2 teaspoons baking powder
- 1 and 1/2 teaspoons baking soda
- 1 teaspoon salt
- 2 large eggs, room temperature
- 3/4 cup whole milk, room temperature
- 1/2 cup vegetable oil
- 2 teaspoons vanilla extract
- 3/4 cup boiling water

For the Cherry Filling:

- 2 cups fresh or canned pitted cherries, drained (reserve juice if using canned)
- 1/4 cup granulated sugar
- 2 tablespoons cornstarch
- 1 tablespoon lemon juice
- 1/4 cup cherry liqueur (optional)

For the Whipped Cream Frosting:

- 2 cups heavy cream, chilled
- 1/2 cup powdered sugar, sifted
- 1 teaspoon vanilla extract

For Decoration (optional):

- Chocolate shavings or curls
- Fresh cherries

Instructions:

1. **Preheat and Prepare:**
    - Preheat your oven to 350°F (175°C). Grease and flour two 9-inch round cake pans, or line them with parchment paper.
2. **Make the Chocolate Sponge Cake:**
    - In a large bowl, sift together the flour, sugar, cocoa powder, baking powder, baking soda, and salt.

- Add the eggs, milk, vegetable oil, and vanilla extract. Beat on medium speed for 2 minutes.
- Stir in the boiling water. The batter will be thin.
- Pour the batter evenly into the prepared cake pans.
- Bake for 30-35 minutes, or until a toothpick inserted into the center comes out clean.
- Remove from the oven and let the cakes cool in the pans for 10 minutes before transferring them to a wire rack to cool completely.

3. **Make the Cherry Filling:**
    - In a saucepan, combine the cherries, sugar, cornstarch, lemon juice, and cherry liqueur (if using).
    - Cook over medium heat, stirring constantly, until the mixture thickens and comes to a boil.
    - Remove from heat and let it cool completely.

4. **Make the Whipped Cream Frosting:**
    - In a chilled bowl, beat the heavy cream, powdered sugar, and vanilla extract until stiff peaks form.

5. **Assemble the Cake:**
    - Place one chocolate sponge cake layer on a serving plate or cake stand.
    - Spread half of the whipped cream frosting evenly over the cake layer.
    - Spoon half of the cherry filling over the whipped cream.
    - Place the second chocolate sponge cake layer on top.
    - Spread the remaining whipped cream frosting over the top and sides of the cake.
    - Spoon the remaining cherry filling over the top of the cake.
    - Optionally, decorate with chocolate shavings or curls and fresh cherries.

6. **Chill and Serve:**
    - Refrigerate the Black Forest Cake for at least 1 hour before serving to allow the flavors to meld together.

7. **Serve:**
    - Slice and serve your delicious Black Forest Cake! It's a delightful combination of chocolate, cherries, and whipped cream.

Tips:

- For an alcohol-free version, you can omit the cherry liqueur or substitute with cherry juice.
- Ensure the heavy cream is well chilled before whipping for best results.
- Store any leftovers covered in the refrigerator for up to 3 days.

Enjoy the indulgent flavors of your homemade Black Forest Cake, a perfect dessert for celebrations and special occasions!

Mocha Cake

Ingredients:

For the Cake:

- 1 and 3/4 cups all-purpose flour
- 3/4 cup unsweetened cocoa powder
- 1 and 1/2 teaspoons baking powder
- 1 and 1/2 teaspoons baking soda
- 1 teaspoon salt
- 2 cups granulated sugar
- 2 large eggs, room temperature
- 1 cup buttermilk, room temperature
- 1/2 cup vegetable oil
- 2 teaspoons vanilla extract
- 1 cup strong brewed coffee, cooled

For the Mocha Buttercream Frosting:

- 1 cup unsalted butter, softened
- 4 cups powdered sugar, sifted
- 1/4 cup unsweetened cocoa powder
- 2-3 tablespoons strong brewed coffee, cooled
- 1 teaspoon vanilla extract
- Pinch of salt

Instructions:

1. **Preheat and Prepare:**
    - Preheat your oven to 350°F (175°C). Grease and flour two 9-inch round cake pans, or line them with parchment paper.
2. **Make the Cake:**
    - In a large bowl, sift together the flour, cocoa powder, baking powder, baking soda, salt, and granulated sugar.
    - Add the eggs, buttermilk, vegetable oil, and vanilla extract. Beat on medium speed for 2 minutes.
    - Gradually add the cooled brewed coffee, mixing until well combined. The batter will be thin.
    - Divide the batter evenly between the prepared cake pans.
    - Bake for 30-35 minutes, or until a toothpick inserted into the center comes out clean.
    - Remove from the oven and let the cakes cool in the pans for 10 minutes before transferring them to a wire rack to cool completely.
3. **Make the Mocha Buttercream Frosting:**

- In a large bowl, beat the softened butter until creamy.
- Gradually add the powdered sugar and cocoa powder, one cup at a time, beating well after each addition.
- Add 2 tablespoons of brewed coffee, vanilla extract, and a pinch of salt. Beat until smooth and creamy. Add more coffee if needed to reach desired consistency.

4. **Assemble the Cake:**
   - Place one cake layer on a serving plate or cake stand.
   - Spread a layer of mocha buttercream frosting over the top.
   - Place the second cake layer on top and frost the top and sides of the cake with the remaining mocha buttercream frosting.

5. **Decorate (optional):**
   - Optionally, decorate with chocolate shavings, cocoa powder dusting, or chocolate-covered coffee beans.

6. **Chill and Serve:**
   - Refrigerate the Mocha Cake for at least 30 minutes before serving to allow the frosting to set.

7. **Serve:**
   - Slice and serve your delicious Mocha Cake! It's perfect for coffee enthusiasts and chocolate lovers alike.

Tips:

- Ensure the brewed coffee is cooled completely before adding it to the cake batter.
- For a stronger coffee flavor, you can add instant espresso powder to the cake batter or frosting.
- Store any leftovers covered in the refrigerator for up to 3 days.

Enjoy the rich and decadent flavors of your homemade Mocha Cake, a delightful dessert for any occasion!

Chiffon Cake

Ingredients:

- 2 and 1/4 cups cake flour
- 1 and 1/2 cups granulated sugar, divided
- 1 tablespoon baking powder
- 1 teaspoon salt
- 1/2 cup vegetable oil
- 7 large eggs, separated, at room temperature
- 3/4 cup water
- 2 teaspoons vanilla extract
- 1/2 teaspoon cream of tartar

Instructions:

1. **Preheat and Prepare:**
   - Preheat your oven to 325°F (160°C). Have an ungreased tube pan (angel food cake pan) ready.
2. **Sift and Mix Dry Ingredients:**
   - In a large bowl, sift together the cake flour, 1 cup of granulated sugar, baking powder, and salt. Make a well in the center.
3. **Mix Wet Ingredients:**
   - In another bowl, whisk together the vegetable oil, egg yolks, water, and vanilla extract until well combined.
4. **Combine Wet and Dry Ingredients:**
   - Gradually pour the wet ingredients into the well of the dry ingredients, whisking until smooth and well combined.
5. **Whip Egg Whites:**
   - In a clean, dry bowl, beat the egg whites and cream of tartar with an electric mixer on medium speed until foamy.
   - Gradually add the remaining 1/2 cup of granulated sugar, a little at a time, while beating on high speed until stiff peaks form.
6. **Fold Egg Whites into Batter:**
   - Gently fold the beaten egg whites into the batter using a rubber spatula. Do this in three additions to ensure the batter is evenly mixed without deflating the egg whites.
7. **Bake:**
   - Pour the batter into the ungreased tube pan.
   - Bake in the preheated oven for 55-60 minutes, or until the top springs back when lightly touched and a toothpick inserted into the center comes out clean.
8. **Cool Invert the Pan:**
   - Immediately upon removing from the oven, invert the tube pan onto a cooling rack. Let the cake cool completely in the pan. This helps the cake maintain its airy structure.

9. **Remove from Pan:**
    - Once completely cool, run a knife around the edges of the pan and the center tube to loosen the cake.
    - Carefully lift the cake out of the pan and place it on a serving plate.
10. **Serve:**
    - Slice and serve your delicious Chiffon Cake as is or with whipped cream and fresh berries.

Tips:

- Ensure the tube pan is ungreased and free from any residue, as the cake needs to cling to the sides as it rises.
- Use cake flour for its finer texture, which contributes to the lightness of the cake.
- Store any leftovers covered at room temperature for up to 3 days.

Enjoy the airy texture and delicate flavor of your homemade Chiffon Cake!

Fruitcake

Ingredients:

- 2 cups mixed dried fruits (such as raisins, currants, chopped apricots, chopped dates, candied cherries, etc.)
- 1 cup chopped nuts (such as walnuts, pecans, almonds, etc.)
- 1/2 cup candied fruit peel, chopped (optional)
- 1 cup unsalted butter, softened
- 1 cup packed brown sugar
- 4 large eggs, room temperature
- 1/4 cup molasses
- 1/4 cup orange juice
- 2 cups all-purpose flour
- 1 teaspoon baking powder
- 1/2 teaspoon baking soda
- 1/2 teaspoon salt
- 1 teaspoon ground cinnamon
- 1/2 teaspoon ground nutmeg
- 1/4 teaspoon ground cloves
- 1/4 teaspoon ground allspice
- 1/2 cup brandy or rum (optional, for soaking)

Instructions:

1. **Prepare the Fruits and Nuts:**
   - In a large bowl, combine the mixed dried fruits, chopped nuts, and candied fruit peel (if using). Toss them together with a tablespoon of flour to coat. This helps prevent them from sinking to the bottom of the cake while baking.
2. **Preheat and Prepare:**
   - Preheat your oven to 325°F (160°C). Grease and flour a 9x5-inch loaf pan, or line it with parchment paper for easier removal.
3. **Make the Batter:**
   - In a separate large bowl, cream together the softened butter and brown sugar until light and fluffy.
   - Beat in the eggs, one at a time, until well combined.
   - Mix in the molasses and orange juice.
4. **Combine Dry Ingredients:**
   - In another bowl, sift together the flour, baking powder, baking soda, salt, cinnamon, nutmeg, cloves, and allspice.
5. **Combine Wet and Dry Ingredients:**
   - Gradually add the dry ingredients to the wet ingredients, mixing until just combined. Do not overmix.
   - Fold in the prepared dried fruits and nuts until evenly distributed in the batter.
6. **Bake the Fruitcake:**

- Pour the batter into the prepared loaf pan, spreading it evenly.
- Bake in the preheated oven for 60-75 minutes, or until a toothpick inserted into the center comes out clean.
- If the top of the cake begins to brown too quickly, cover it loosely with aluminum foil during the last 15-20 minutes of baking.

7. **Cool and Soak (optional):**
    - Remove the fruitcake from the oven and let it cool in the pan for 10 minutes before transferring it to a wire rack to cool completely.
    - If desired, you can poke holes in the top of the cake with a toothpick and drizzle 1/4 cup of brandy or rum over the warm cake. Let it soak in as the cake cools.

8. **Store:**
    - Once completely cooled and optionally soaked, wrap the fruitcake tightly in plastic wrap or store it in an airtight container.
    - For best flavor, let the fruitcake sit at room temperature for a day or two before serving. It can be stored at room temperature for up to 1 week or refrigerated for longer storage.

Tips:

- Customize the dried fruits and nuts to your preference. Some popular additions include dried cranberries, figs, and hazelnuts.
- For a richer flavor, soak the dried fruits in brandy or rum overnight before using in the recipe.
- Fruitcake improves with age and can be made several weeks in advance of serving.

Enjoy the rich, fruity flavors and warm spices of your homemade Fruitcake, perfect for festive occasions!

Tiramisu Cake

Ingredients:

For the Sponge Cake:

- 1 and 1/2 cups cake flour
- 1 and 1/2 teaspoons baking powder
- 1/2 teaspoon baking soda
- 1/2 teaspoon salt
- 1/2 cup unsalted butter, softened
- 1 cup granulated sugar
- 3 large eggs, room temperature
- 1 teaspoon vanilla extract
- 1/2 cup buttermilk, room temperature
- 1/4 cup brewed espresso or strong coffee, cooled

For the Coffee Soaking Syrup:

- 1/2 cup brewed espresso or strong coffee, cooled
- 2 tablespoons coffee liqueur (optional)
- 2 tablespoons granulated sugar

For the Mascarpone Filling:

- 16 oz mascarpone cheese, softened
- 1 cup powdered sugar, sifted
- 1 and 1/2 cups heavy cream, chilled
- 1 teaspoon vanilla extract

For Garnish:

- Cocoa powder, for dusting
- Chocolate shavings or curls

Instructions:

1. **Preheat and Prepare:**
    - Preheat your oven to 350°F (175°C). Grease and flour two 8-inch round cake pans, or line them with parchment paper.
2. **Make the Sponge Cake:**
    - In a medium bowl, sift together the cake flour, baking powder, baking soda, and salt.
    - In a large bowl, cream together the softened butter and granulated sugar until light and fluffy.

- Add the eggs one at a time, beating well after each addition. Mix in the vanilla extract.
- Gradually add the dry ingredients to the creamed mixture, alternating with the buttermilk. Begin and end with the dry ingredients, mixing until just combined.
- Stir in the brewed espresso or coffee until evenly incorporated.
- Divide the batter evenly between the prepared cake pans.
- Bake for 20-25 minutes, or until a toothpick inserted into the center comes out clean.
- Remove from the oven and let the cakes cool in the pans for 10 minutes before transferring them to a wire rack to cool completely.

3. **Make the Coffee Soaking Syrup:**
   - In a small bowl, stir together the brewed espresso or coffee, coffee liqueur (if using), and granulated sugar until the sugar is dissolved. Set aside.

4. **Make the Mascarpone Filling:**
   - In a large bowl, beat the softened mascarpone cheese and powdered sugar until smooth and creamy.
   - In another bowl, whip the chilled heavy cream and vanilla extract until stiff peaks form.
   - Gently fold the whipped cream into the mascarpone mixture until well combined and smooth. Be careful not to deflate the mixture.

5. **Assemble the Tiramisu Cake:**
   - Place one cooled sponge cake layer on a serving plate or cake stand.
   - Brush the top of the cake layer generously with the coffee soaking syrup, allowing it to absorb.
   - Spread half of the mascarpone filling evenly over the soaked cake layer.
   - Place the second sponge cake layer on top and repeat the soaking process with the remaining coffee syrup.
   - Spread the remaining mascarpone filling over the top and sides of the cake, smoothing it with a spatula.

6. **Decorate and Chill:**
   - Dust the top of the Tiramisu Cake with cocoa powder and garnish with chocolate shavings or curls.
   - Refrigerate the cake for at least 4 hours, or preferably overnight, to allow the flavors to meld together and for the cake to set.

7. **Serve:**
   - Slice and serve your delicious Tiramisu Cake chilled. It's perfect for coffee lovers and special occasions!

Tips:

- Ensure the mascarpone cheese is softened at room temperature for easy blending.
- For a non-alcoholic version, omit the coffee liqueur in the soaking syrup.
- Store any leftovers covered in the refrigerator for up to 3 days.

Enjoy the rich and creamy layers of your homemade Tiramisu Cake, a decadent twist on a classic dessert!

Angel Food Cake

Ingredients:

For the Sponge Cake:

- 1 and 1/2 cups cake flour
- 1 and 1/2 teaspoons baking powder
- 1/2 teaspoon baking soda
- 1/2 teaspoon salt
- 1/2 cup unsalted butter, softened
- 1 cup granulated sugar
- 3 large eggs, room temperature
- 1 teaspoon vanilla extract
- 1/2 cup buttermilk, room temperature
- 1/4 cup brewed espresso or strong coffee, cooled

For the Coffee Soaking Syrup:

- 1/2 cup brewed espresso or strong coffee, cooled
- 2 tablespoons coffee liqueur (optional)
- 2 tablespoons granulated sugar

For the Mascarpone Filling:

- 16 oz mascarpone cheese, softened
- 1 cup powdered sugar, sifted
- 1 and 1/2 cups heavy cream, chilled
- 1 teaspoon vanilla extract

For Garnish:

- Cocoa powder, for dusting
- Chocolate shavings or curls

Instructions:

1. **Preheat and Prepare:**
   - Preheat your oven to 350°F (175°C). Grease and flour two 8-inch round cake pans, or line them with parchment paper.
2. **Make the Sponge Cake:**
   - In a medium bowl, sift together the cake flour, baking powder, baking soda, and salt.
   - In a large bowl, cream together the softened butter and granulated sugar until light and fluffy.

- Add the eggs one at a time, beating well after each addition. Mix in the vanilla extract.
- Gradually add the dry ingredients to the creamed mixture, alternating with the buttermilk. Begin and end with the dry ingredients, mixing until just combined.
- Stir in the brewed espresso or coffee until evenly incorporated.
- Divide the batter evenly between the prepared cake pans.
- Bake for 20-25 minutes, or until a toothpick inserted into the center comes out clean.
- Remove from the oven and let the cakes cool in the pans for 10 minutes before transferring them to a wire rack to cool completely.

3. **Make the Coffee Soaking Syrup:**
   - In a small bowl, stir together the brewed espresso or coffee, coffee liqueur (if using), and granulated sugar until the sugar is dissolved. Set aside.

4. **Make the Mascarpone Filling:**
   - In a large bowl, beat the softened mascarpone cheese and powdered sugar until smooth and creamy.
   - In another bowl, whip the chilled heavy cream and vanilla extract until stiff peaks form.
   - Gently fold the whipped cream into the mascarpone mixture until well combined and smooth. Be careful not to deflate the mixture.

5. **Assemble the Tiramisu Cake:**
   - Place one cooled sponge cake layer on a serving plate or cake stand.
   - Brush the top of the cake layer generously with the coffee soaking syrup, allowing it to absorb.
   - Spread half of the mascarpone filling evenly over the soaked cake layer.
   - Place the second sponge cake layer on top and repeat the soaking process with the remaining coffee syrup.
   - Spread the remaining mascarpone filling over the top and sides of the cake, smoothing it with a spatula.

6. **Decorate and Chill:**
   - Dust the top of the Tiramisu Cake with cocoa powder and garnish with chocolate shavings or curls.
   - Refrigerate the cake for at least 4 hours, or preferably overnight, to allow the flavors to meld together and for the cake to set.

7. **Serve:**
   - Slice and serve your delicious Tiramisu Cake chilled. It's perfect for coffee lovers and special occasions!

Tips:

- Ensure the mascarpone cheese is softened at room temperature for easy blending.
- For a non-alcoholic version, omit the coffee liqueur in the soaking syrup.
- Store any leftovers covered in the refrigerator for up to 3 days.

Enjoy the rich and creamy layers of your homemade Tiramisu Cake, a decadent twist on a classic dessert!

Angel Food Cake

Ingredients:

- 1 cup cake flour
- 1 and 1/2 cups granulated sugar, divided
- 12 large egg whites, at room temperature
- 1 teaspoon cream of tartar
- 1/4 teaspoon salt
- 1 teaspoon vanilla extract
- 1/2 teaspoon almond extract (optional)
- Fresh berries and whipped cream, for serving (optional)

Instructions:

1. **Preheat and Prepare:**
   - Preheat your oven to 350°F (175°C). Have an ungreased angel food cake pan (tube pan) ready.
2. **Sift and Mix Dry Ingredients:**
   - In a medium bowl, sift together the cake flour and 1/2 cup of granulated sugar. Set aside.
3. **Whip Egg Whites:**
   - In a large bowl or the bowl of a stand mixer, beat the egg whites on medium speed until frothy.
   - Add the cream of tartar and salt. Increase the speed to medium-high and continue beating until soft peaks form.
   - Gradually add the remaining 1 cup of granulated sugar, about 2 tablespoons at a time, while beating on high speed. Continue to beat until stiff peaks form and the egg whites are glossy.
4. **Fold in Flavorings and Flour Mixture:**
   - Gently fold in the vanilla extract and almond extract (if using) into the whipped egg whites.
   - Gradually sift and fold the sifted flour mixture into the egg white mixture in 3-4 additions, folding gently until just combined. Do not overmix.
5. **Bake:**
   - Spoon the batter into the ungreased angel food cake pan and smooth the top with a spatula.
   - Bake in the preheated oven for 35-40 minutes, or until the top is golden brown and springs back when lightly touched.
   - Remove from the oven and immediately invert the pan onto a cooling rack, placing the center tube over the neck of a bottle or on its built-in feet (if your pan has them). Let the cake cool completely upside down in the pan. This helps prevent the cake from collapsing.
6. **Remove from Pan:**

- Once completely cool, run a knife around the edges of the pan and the center tube to loosen the cake.
- Carefully lift the cake out of the pan and place it on a serving plate.
7. **Serve:**
    - Slice and serve your delicious Angel Food Cake as is or with fresh berries and whipped cream.

Tips:

- Use cake flour for its fine texture, which helps create a lighter cake.
- Ensure the angel food cake pan is ungreased and clean, as the cake needs to cling to the sides as it rises.
- Store any leftovers covered at room temperature for up to 2 days.

Enjoy the light and fluffy texture of your homemade Angel Food Cake, perfect for a simple and elegant dessert!

Bundt Cake

Ingredients:

- 3 cups all-purpose flour
- 1 teaspoon baking powder
- 1/2 teaspoon baking soda
- 1/2 teaspoon salt
- 1 cup unsalted butter, softened
- 2 cups granulated sugar
- 4 large eggs, room temperature
- 1 tablespoon vanilla extract
- 1 cup buttermilk, room temperature

Instructions:

1. **Preheat and Prepare:**
    - Preheat your oven to 350°F (175°C). Grease and flour a 10-cup Bundt pan, ensuring all crevices are well coated.
2. **Mix Dry Ingredients:**
    - In a medium bowl, sift together the flour, baking powder, baking soda, and salt. Set aside.
3. **Cream Butter and Sugar:**
    - In a large bowl or the bowl of a stand mixer, cream together the softened butter and granulated sugar until light and fluffy.
4. **Add Eggs and Vanilla:**
    - Beat in the eggs one at a time, mixing well after each addition. Stir in the vanilla extract.
5. **Alternate Adding Dry and Wet Ingredients:**
    - Gradually add the dry ingredients to the creamed mixture, alternating with the buttermilk. Begin and end with the dry ingredients, mixing until just combined. Do not overmix.
6. **Bake:**
    - Spoon the batter into the prepared Bundt pan, spreading it evenly with a spatula.
    - Bake in the preheated oven for 45-50 minutes, or until a toothpick inserted into the center comes out clean.
7. **Cool and Remove from Pan:**
    - Remove the cake from the oven and let it cool in the pan for 10 minutes.
    - Invert the Bundt pan onto a wire rack and gently lift the pan to release the cake. Let the cake cool completely on the wire rack.
8. **Optional Glaze or Dusting:**
    - Once cooled, you can dust the Bundt cake with powdered sugar or drizzle with a simple glaze of powdered sugar mixed with milk or lemon juice for extra sweetness.
9. **Serve:**

- Slice and serve your delicious Vanilla Bundt Cake as is, or with fresh berries and whipped cream if desired.

Tips:

- Ensure your Bundt pan is well-greased and floured to prevent sticking.
- Use room temperature ingredients for better incorporation into the batter.
- Store any leftovers covered at room temperature for up to 3 days.

Enjoy the moist and flavorful simplicity of your homemade Vanilla Bundt Cake, perfect for any occasion!

Lemon Poppy Seed Cake

Ingredients:

For the Cake:

- 1 and 1/2 cups all-purpose flour
- 2 tablespoons poppy seeds
- 1 teaspoon baking powder
- 1/2 teaspoon baking soda
- 1/4 teaspoon salt
- 1/2 cup unsalted butter, softened
- 1 cup granulated sugar
- 2 large eggs, room temperature
- 1 teaspoon vanilla extract
- Zest of 2 lemons
- 1/4 cup fresh lemon juice
- 1/2 cup sour cream or Greek yogurt

For the Lemon Glaze:

- 1 cup powdered sugar
- 2-3 tablespoons fresh lemon juice
- Zest of 1 lemon (optional, for garnish)

Instructions:

1. **Preheat and Prepare:**
    - Preheat your oven to 350°F (175°C). Grease and flour a 9x5-inch loaf pan or prepare with parchment paper for easier removal.
2. **Mix Dry Ingredients:**
    - In a medium bowl, whisk together the flour, poppy seeds, baking powder, baking soda, and salt. Set aside.
3. **Cream Butter and Sugar:**
    - In a large bowl or the bowl of a stand mixer, cream together the softened butter and granulated sugar until light and fluffy.
4. **Add Eggs and Flavorings:**
    - Beat in the eggs, one at a time, mixing well after each addition. Add the vanilla extract, lemon zest, and lemon juice, mixing until combined.
5. **Alternate Adding Dry and Wet Ingredients:**
    - Gradually add the dry ingredients to the creamed mixture, alternating with the sour cream or Greek yogurt. Begin and end with the dry ingredients, mixing until just combined. Do not overmix.
6. **Bake:**
    - Pour the batter into the prepared loaf pan, spreading it evenly with a spatula.

- Bake in the preheated oven for 45-50 minutes, or until a toothpick inserted into the center comes out clean.

7. **Cool and Glaze:**
    - Remove the cake from the oven and let it cool in the pan for 10 minutes.
    - Carefully remove the cake from the pan and place it on a wire rack to cool completely.
8. **Make the Lemon Glaze:**
    - In a small bowl, whisk together the powdered sugar and lemon juice until smooth and pourable.
    - Drizzle the glaze over the cooled cake. Sprinkle with additional lemon zest for garnish, if desired.
9. **Serve:**
    - Slice and serve your delicious Lemon Poppy Seed Cake. Enjoy the bright flavors and tender crumb!

Tips:

- Ensure all ingredients are at room temperature for easier mixing and better incorporation.
- Adjust the amount of lemon juice in the glaze to achieve your desired consistency.
- Store any leftovers covered at room temperature for up to 3 days.

This Lemon Poppy Seed Cake is perfect for brunches, afternoon teas, or as a delightful dessert any time of the year!

Spice Cake

Ingredients:

- 2 cups all-purpose flour
- 1 teaspoon baking powder
- 1/2 teaspoon baking soda
- 1/2 teaspoon salt
- 1 teaspoon ground cinnamon
- 1/2 teaspoon ground nutmeg
- 1/2 teaspoon ground cloves
- 1/2 cup unsalted butter, softened
- 1 cup granulated sugar
- 1/2 cup packed light brown sugar
- 2 large eggs, room temperature
- 1 teaspoon vanilla extract
- 1 cup buttermilk, room temperature

Instructions:

1. **Preheat and Prepare:**
   - Preheat your oven to 350°F (175°C). Grease and flour a 9x13-inch baking pan or two 8-inch round cake pans.
2. **Mix Dry Ingredients:**
   - In a medium bowl, whisk together the flour, baking powder, baking soda, salt, cinnamon, nutmeg, and cloves. Set aside.
3. **Cream Butter and Sugars:**
   - In a large bowl or the bowl of a stand mixer, cream together the softened butter, granulated sugar, and brown sugar until light and fluffy.
4. **Add Eggs and Vanilla:**
   - Beat in the eggs one at a time, mixing well after each addition. Stir in the vanilla extract.
5. **Alternate Adding Dry and Wet Ingredients:**
   - Gradually add the dry ingredients to the creamed mixture, alternating with the buttermilk. Begin and end with the dry ingredients, mixing until just combined. Do not overmix.
6. **Bake:**
   - Pour the batter into the prepared baking pan(s), spreading it evenly with a spatula.
   - Bake in the preheated oven for 30-35 minutes (for a 9x13-inch pan) or 25-30 minutes (for round pans), or until a toothpick inserted into the center comes out clean.
7. **Cool and Frost (optional):**
   - Remove the cake from the oven and let it cool in the pan(s) for 10 minutes.

- Carefully remove the cake from the pan(s) and place it on a wire rack to cool completely.

Rhubarb Cake

Ingredients:

For the Cake:

- 1 cup granulated sugar
- 1/2 cup unsalted butter, softened
- 1 large egg
- 1 teaspoon vanilla extract
- 1 cup sour cream
- 2 cups all-purpose flour
- 1 teaspoon baking soda
- 1/2 teaspoon salt
- 2 cups fresh rhubarb, diced

For the Topping:

- 1/2 cup granulated sugar
- 1 teaspoon ground cinnamon

Instructions:

1. **Preheat and Prepare:**
    - Preheat your oven to 350°F (175°C). Grease a 9x13-inch baking dish.
2. **Mix Wet Ingredients:**
    - In a large bowl, cream together the sugar and softened butter until light and fluffy. Add the egg and vanilla extract, mixing well.
3. **Add Sour Cream:**
    - Stir in the sour cream until well combined.
4. **Combine Dry Ingredients:**
    - In a separate bowl, whisk together the flour, baking soda, and salt.
5. **Combine Wet and Dry Ingredients:**
    - Gradually add the dry ingredients to the wet mixture, mixing until just combined.
6. **Fold in Rhubarb:**
    - Gently fold in the diced rhubarb until evenly distributed in the batter.
7. **Prepare Topping:**
    - In a small bowl, mix together the sugar and ground cinnamon for the topping.
8. **Assemble and Bake:**
    - Spread the batter evenly into the prepared baking dish.
    - Sprinkle the cinnamon-sugar topping evenly over the batter.
9. **Bake:**
    - Bake in the preheated oven for 35-40 minutes, or until a toothpick inserted into the center comes out clean and the top is golden brown.
10. **Cool and Serve:**

- Allow the cake to cool in the pan on a wire rack for at least 15-20 minutes before slicing and serving.

Tips:

- Ensure the rhubarb is diced into small pieces to ensure even distribution throughout the cake.
- Serve warm or at room temperature, optionally with a dollop of whipped cream or vanilla ice cream.

This Rhubarb Cake is perfect for showcasing the tartness of fresh rhubarb in a delicious dessert. Enjoy!

Pistachio Cake

Ingredients:

For the Cake:

- 1 cup unsalted shelled pistachios, finely ground
- 1 and 1/2 cups cake flour
- 2 teaspoons baking powder
- 1/2 teaspoon baking soda
- 1/4 teaspoon salt
- 1/2 cup unsalted butter, softened
- 1 cup granulated sugar
- 2 large eggs, room temperature
- 1 teaspoon vanilla extract
- 1 cup buttermilk, room temperature
- Green food coloring (optional)

For the Pistachio Buttercream Frosting:

- 1 cup unsalted butter, softened
- 2 cups powdered sugar, sifted
- 1/2 cup unsalted shelled pistachios, finely ground
- 1 teaspoon vanilla extract
- Green food coloring (optional)

Instructions:

1. **Preheat and Prepare:**
    - Preheat your oven to 350°F (175°C). Grease and flour two 9-inch round cake pans, or line them with parchment paper.
2. **Prepare Pistachios:**
    - Finely grind the shelled pistachios in a food processor until they resemble coarse crumbs. Measure out 1 cup for the cake and reserve 1/2 cup for the frosting.
3. **Mix Dry Ingredients:**
    - In a medium bowl, whisk together the finely ground pistachios, cake flour, baking powder, baking soda, and salt. Set aside.
4. **Cream Butter and Sugar:**
    - In a large bowl or the bowl of a stand mixer, cream together the softened butter and granulated sugar until light and fluffy.
5. **Add Eggs and Vanilla:**
    - Beat in the eggs one at a time, mixing well after each addition. Stir in the vanilla extract.
6. **Alternate Adding Dry and Wet Ingredients:**

- Gradually add the dry ingredients to the creamed mixture, alternating with the buttermilk. Begin and end with the dry ingredients, mixing until just combined. Add a few drops of green food coloring, if desired, to enhance the color.

7. **Bake:**
   - Divide the batter evenly between the prepared cake pans and smooth the tops with a spatula.
   - Bake in the preheated oven for 25-30 minutes, or until a toothpick inserted into the center comes out clean.

8. **Cool and Frost:**
   - Remove the cakes from the oven and let them cool in the pans for 10 minutes before transferring them to a wire rack to cool completely.

9. **Make Pistachio Buttercream Frosting:**
   - In a large bowl, beat the softened butter until creamy. Gradually add the powdered sugar, beating until light and fluffy.
   - Mix in the finely ground pistachios and vanilla extract. Add a few drops of green food coloring, if desired, for a more vibrant green color.

10. **Assemble the Cake:**
    - Place one cake layer on a serving plate or cake stand. Spread a layer of pistachio buttercream frosting evenly over the top.
    - Place the second cake layer on top and frost the top and sides of the cake with the remaining pistachio buttercream frosting.

11. **Decorate (optional):**
    - Garnish the cake with additional finely ground pistachios or whole pistachios for decoration.

12. **Chill and Serve:**
    - Chill the cake in the refrigerator for about 30 minutes to allow the frosting to set before slicing and serving.

Tips:

- Ensure the pistachios are finely ground to incorporate smoothly into both the cake batter and frosting.
- If you prefer a less pronounced green color, you can omit the food coloring.
- Store the cake covered in the refrigerator. Bring to room temperature before serving for the best flavor and texture.

Enjoy the deliciously nutty and flavorful Pistachio Cake, perfect for special occasions or as a delightful treat!

Mango Cake

Ingredients:

For the Cake:

- 2 cups all-purpose flour
- 2 teaspoons baking powder
- 1/2 teaspoon baking soda
- 1/4 teaspoon salt
- 1/2 cup unsalted butter, softened
- 1 cup granulated sugar
- 2 large eggs, room temperature
- 1 teaspoon vanilla extract
- 1 cup mango puree (from ripe mangoes)
- 1/2 cup buttermilk, room temperature

For the Mango Buttercream Frosting:

- 1 cup unsalted butter, softened
- 4 cups powdered sugar, sifted
- 1/2 cup mango puree
- 1 teaspoon vanilla extract
- Fresh mango slices or mango chunks for garnish (optional)

Instructions:

1. **Preheat and Prepare:**
   - Preheat your oven to 350°F (175°C). Grease and flour two 9-inch round cake pans, or line them with parchment paper.
2. **Prepare Mango Puree:**
   - Peel and dice ripe mangoes. Puree the mango flesh in a blender or food processor until smooth. Measure out 1 cup of mango puree for the cake and 1/2 cup for the frosting. Set aside.
3. **Mix Dry Ingredients:**
   - In a medium bowl, whisk together the flour, baking powder, baking soda, and salt. Set aside.
4. **Cream Butter and Sugar:**
   - In a large bowl or the bowl of a stand mixer, cream together the softened butter and granulated sugar until light and fluffy.
5. **Add Eggs and Vanilla:**
   - Beat in the eggs one at a time, mixing well after each addition. Stir in the vanilla extract.
6. **Add Mango Puree and Buttermilk:**

- Mix in the mango puree until well combined. Gradually add the dry ingredients to the creamed mixture, alternating with the buttermilk. Begin and end with the dry ingredients, mixing until just combined. Do not overmix.

7. **Bake:**
   - Divide the batter evenly between the prepared cake pans and smooth the tops with a spatula.
   - Bake in the preheated oven for 25-30 minutes, or until a toothpick inserted into the center comes out clean.

8. **Cool and Prepare Frosting:**
   - Remove the cakes from the oven and let them cool in the pans for 10 minutes before transferring them to a wire rack to cool completely.

9. **Make Mango Buttercream Frosting:**
   - In a large bowl, beat the softened butter until creamy. Gradually add the powdered sugar, beating until light and fluffy.
   - Mix in the mango puree and vanilla extract until smooth and well combined.

10. **Assemble the Cake:**
    - Place one cake layer on a serving plate or cake stand. Spread a layer of mango buttercream frosting evenly over the top.
    - Place the second cake layer on top and frost the top and sides of the cake with the remaining mango buttercream frosting.

11. **Decorate (optional):**
    - Garnish the cake with fresh mango slices or chunks for a vibrant and tropical look.

12. **Chill and Serve:**
    - Chill the cake in the refrigerator for about 30 minutes to allow the frosting to set before slicing and serving.

Tips:

- Use ripe mangoes for the best flavor and sweetness in both the cake and frosting.
- Adjust the consistency of the frosting with more powdered sugar for a thicker consistency or more mango puree for a smoother texture.
- Store the cake covered in the refrigerator. Bring to room temperature before serving for the best flavor and texture.

Enjoy the tropical delight of Mango Cake, perfect for any celebration or as a refreshing dessert!

Orange Cake

Ingredients:

For the Cake:

- 2 cups all-purpose flour
- 2 teaspoons baking powder
- 1/2 teaspoon baking soda
- 1/4 teaspoon salt
- 1 cup unsalted butter, softened
- 1 and 1/4 cups granulated sugar
- 3 large eggs, room temperature
- 1 teaspoon vanilla extract
- Zest of 2 oranges
- 1/2 cup fresh orange juice (from about 2-3 oranges)
- 1/2 cup buttermilk, room temperature

For the Orange Glaze:

- 1 cup powdered sugar
- 2-3 tablespoons fresh orange juice
- Zest of 1 orange (optional, for garnish)

Instructions:

1. **Preheat and Prepare:**
    - Preheat your oven to 350°F (175°C). Grease and flour a 9x13-inch baking pan, or line it with parchment paper.
2. **Mix Dry Ingredients:**
    - In a medium bowl, whisk together the flour, baking powder, baking soda, and salt. Set aside.
3. **Cream Butter and Sugar:**
    - In a large bowl or the bowl of a stand mixer, cream together the softened butter and granulated sugar until light and fluffy.
4. **Add Eggs and Flavorings:**
    - Beat in the eggs one at a time, mixing well after each addition. Stir in the vanilla extract and orange zest.
5. **Combine Orange Juice and Buttermilk:**
    - In a small bowl, combine the fresh orange juice and buttermilk.
6. **Alternate Adding Dry and Wet Ingredients:**
    - Gradually add the dry ingredients to the creamed mixture, alternating with the orange juice/buttermilk mixture. Begin and end with the dry ingredients, mixing until just combined. Do not overmix.
7. **Bake:**

- Pour the batter into the prepared baking pan, spreading it evenly with a spatula.
- Bake in the preheated oven for 25-30 minutes, or until a toothpick inserted into the center comes out clean.

8. **Cool and Glaze:**
   - Remove the cake from the oven and let it cool in the pan for 10 minutes.
   - In a small bowl, whisk together the powdered sugar and fresh orange juice until smooth. Adjust the consistency by adding more juice or sugar as needed.

9. **Glaze the Cake:**
   - Pierce the warm cake with a fork or toothpick all over the top. Pour the orange glaze evenly over the cake, allowing it to soak in.

10. **Garnish (optional):**
    - Sprinkle with additional orange zest for a burst of color and extra orange flavor.

11. **Cool Completely and Serve:**
    - Allow the cake to cool completely in the pan on a wire rack before slicing and serving.

Tips:

- Use fresh oranges for the best flavor in both the cake and glaze.
- Adjust the sweetness of the glaze to your preference by adding more or less powdered sugar.
- Store any leftovers covered at room temperature for up to 3 days.

Enjoy the fresh and citrusy taste of Orange Cake, perfect for any occasion or as a delightful treat!

Pear Cake

Ingredients:

For the Cake:

- 2 cups all-purpose flour
- 1 teaspoon baking powder
- 1/2 teaspoon baking soda
- 1/2 teaspoon salt
- 1/2 cup unsalted butter, softened
- 1 cup granulated sugar
- 2 large eggs, room temperature
- 1 teaspoon vanilla extract
- 1/2 cup sour cream or plain yogurt
- 3 ripe pears, peeled, cored, and diced

For the Streusel Topping:

- 1/4 cup all-purpose flour
- 1/4 cup granulated sugar
- 2 tablespoons unsalted butter, cold and cut into small pieces
- 1/2 teaspoon ground cinnamon

Instructions:

1. **Preheat and Prepare:**
   - Preheat your oven to 350°F (175°C). Grease and flour a 9x9-inch baking pan, or line it with parchment paper.
2. **Mix Dry Ingredients:**
   - In a medium bowl, whisk together the flour, baking powder, baking soda, and salt. Set aside.
3. **Cream Butter and Sugar:**
   - In a large bowl or the bowl of a stand mixer, cream together the softened butter and granulated sugar until light and fluffy.
4. **Add Eggs and Vanilla:**
   - Beat in the eggs one at a time, mixing well after each addition. Stir in the vanilla extract.
5. **Add Sour Cream or Yogurt:**
   - Mix in the sour cream or yogurt until well combined.
6. **Combine Wet and Dry Ingredients:**
   - Gradually add the dry ingredients to the creamed mixture, mixing until just combined.
7. **Fold in Pears:**
   - Gently fold in the diced pears until evenly distributed in the batter.

8. **Make Streusel Topping:**
   - In a small bowl, combine the flour, sugar, cold butter pieces, and ground cinnamon. Use a fork or pastry blender to mix until crumbly and the butter is pea-sized.
9. **Assemble and Bake:**
   - Spread the cake batter evenly into the prepared baking pan.
   - Sprinkle the streusel topping evenly over the batter.
10. **Bake:**
    - Bake in the preheated oven for 40-45 minutes, or until a toothpick inserted into the center comes out clean and the top is golden brown.
11. **Cool and Serve:**
    - Remove the cake from the oven and let it cool in the pan for 10 minutes.
    - Carefully transfer the cake to a wire rack to cool completely before slicing and serving.

Tips:

- Choose ripe but firm pears for the best texture in the cake.
- If you prefer, you can add a teaspoon of ground cinnamon or nutmeg to the cake batter for extra flavor.
- Serve the Pear Cake warm or at room temperature. It pairs wonderfully with a dollop of whipped cream or vanilla ice cream.

Enjoy this delightful Pear Cake as a comforting dessert or a sweet treat with afternoon tea!

Fig Cake

Ingredients:

For the Cake:

- 1 and 1/2 cups all-purpose flour
- 1 teaspoon baking powder
- 1/2 teaspoon baking soda
- 1/4 teaspoon salt
- 1/2 cup unsalted butter, softened
- 3/4 cup granulated sugar
- 2 large eggs, room temperature
- 1 teaspoon vanilla extract
- 1/2 cup sour cream or plain yogurt
- 1 cup fresh figs, chopped (about 8-10 figs)

For the Fig Jam Glaze:

- 1/2 cup fig jam
- 2 tablespoons water

Instructions:

1. **Preheat and Prepare:**
    - Preheat your oven to 350°F (175°C). Grease and flour a 9-inch round cake pan, or line it with parchment paper.
2. **Mix Dry Ingredients:**
    - In a medium bowl, whisk together the flour, baking powder, baking soda, and salt. Set aside.
3. **Cream Butter and Sugar:**
    - In a large bowl or the bowl of a stand mixer, cream together the softened butter and granulated sugar until light and fluffy.
4. **Add Eggs and Vanilla:**
    - Beat in the eggs one at a time, mixing well after each addition. Stir in the vanilla extract.
5. **Add Sour Cream or Yogurt:**
    - Mix in the sour cream or yogurt until well combined.
6. **Combine Wet and Dry Ingredients:**
    - Gradually add the dry ingredients to the creamed mixture, mixing until just combined.
7. **Fold in Chopped Figs:**
    - Gently fold in the chopped figs until evenly distributed in the batter.
8. **Bake:**
    - Spread the cake batter evenly into the prepared cake pan.

- Bake in the preheated oven for 30-35 minutes, or until a toothpick inserted into the center comes out clean and the top is golden brown.

9. **Cool and Glaze:**
    - Remove the cake from the oven and let it cool in the pan for 10 minutes.
    - In a small saucepan, heat the fig jam and water over low heat until the jam is melted and smooth.

10. **Glaze the Cake:**
    - Pierce the warm cake all over with a fork or toothpick. Brush the warm fig jam glaze evenly over the top of the cake.

11. **Cool Completely and Serve:**
    - Allow the cake to cool completely in the pan on a wire rack before slicing and serving.

Tips:

- Use fresh figs for the best flavor in this cake. You can also use dried figs that have been rehydrated in warm water and chopped.
- Adjust the sweetness of the glaze by adding more or less fig jam according to your taste.
- Serve the Fig Cake at room temperature. It pairs well with a cup of tea or coffee.

Enjoy this Fig Cake, which showcases the natural sweetness and richness of figs in every bite!

Plum Cake

Ingredients:

For the Cake:

- 1 and 1/2 cups all-purpose flour
- 1 and 1/2 teaspoons baking powder
- 1/4 teaspoon baking soda
- 1/4 teaspoon salt
- 1/2 cup unsalted butter, softened
- 3/4 cup granulated sugar
- 2 large eggs, room temperature
- 1 teaspoon vanilla extract
- 1/2 cup sour cream or plain yogurt
- 3-4 ripe plums, pitted and sliced (about 2 cups sliced plums)

For the Streusel Topping:

- 1/4 cup all-purpose flour
- 1/4 cup granulated sugar
- 2 tablespoons unsalted butter, cold and cut into small pieces
- 1/2 teaspoon ground cinnamon

Instructions:

1. **Preheat and Prepare:**
    - Preheat your oven to 350°F (175°C). Grease and flour a 9-inch round cake pan, or line it with parchment paper.
2. **Mix Dry Ingredients:**
    - In a medium bowl, whisk together the flour, baking powder, baking soda, and salt. Set aside.
3. **Cream Butter and Sugar:**
    - In a large bowl or the bowl of a stand mixer, cream together the softened butter and granulated sugar until light and fluffy.
4. **Add Eggs and Vanilla:**
    - Beat in the eggs one at a time, mixing well after each addition. Stir in the vanilla extract.
5. **Add Sour Cream or Yogurt:**
    - Mix in the sour cream or yogurt until well combined.
6. **Combine Wet and Dry Ingredients:**
    - Gradually add the dry ingredients to the creamed mixture, mixing until just combined.
7. **Prepare Streusel Topping:**

- In a small bowl, combine the flour, sugar, cold butter pieces, and ground cinnamon. Use a fork or pastry blender to mix until crumbly and the butter is pea-sized.

8. **Assemble and Bake:**
    - Spread the cake batter evenly into the prepared cake pan.
    - Arrange the sliced plums on top of the batter in a decorative pattern.
    - Sprinkle the streusel topping evenly over the plums.
9. **Bake:**
    - Bake in the preheated oven for 30-35 minutes, or until a toothpick inserted into the center comes out clean and the top is golden brown.
10. **Cool and Serve:**
    - Remove the cake from the oven and let it cool in the pan for 10 minutes.
    - Carefully transfer the cake to a wire rack to cool completely before slicing and serving.

Tips:

- Use ripe but firm plums for the best texture in the cake.
- If desired, sprinkle some sliced almonds or chopped nuts over the streusel topping before baking for added crunch.
- Serve the Plum Cake warm or at room temperature. It's delicious on its own or with a dollop of whipped cream or vanilla ice cream.

Enjoy this delightful Plum Cake, perfect for showcasing the flavors of fresh, seasonal plums!

Apricot Cake

Ingredients:

For the Cake:

- 1 and 1/2 cups all-purpose flour
- 1 and 1/2 teaspoons baking powder
- 1/4 teaspoon baking soda
- 1/4 teaspoon salt
- 1/2 cup unsalted butter, softened
- 3/4 cup granulated sugar
- 2 large eggs, room temperature
- 1 teaspoon vanilla extract
- 1/2 cup sour cream or plain yogurt
- 1 and 1/2 cups fresh apricots, pitted and sliced

For the Streusel Topping:

- 1/4 cup all-purpose flour
- 1/4 cup granulated sugar
- 2 tablespoons unsalted butter, cold and cut into small pieces
- 1/2 teaspoon ground cinnamon

Instructions:

1. **Preheat and Prepare:**
    - Preheat your oven to 350°F (175°C). Grease and flour a 9-inch round cake pan, or line it with parchment paper.
2. **Mix Dry Ingredients:**
    - In a medium bowl, whisk together the flour, baking powder, baking soda, and salt. Set aside.
3. **Cream Butter and Sugar:**
    - In a large bowl or the bowl of a stand mixer, cream together the softened butter and granulated sugar until light and fluffy.
4. **Add Eggs and Vanilla:**
    - Beat in the eggs one at a time, mixing well after each addition. Stir in the vanilla extract.
5. **Add Sour Cream or Yogurt:**
    - Mix in the sour cream or yogurt until well combined.
6. **Combine Wet and Dry Ingredients:**
    - Gradually add the dry ingredients to the creamed mixture, mixing until just combined.
7. **Prepare Streusel Topping:**

- In a small bowl, combine the flour, sugar, cold butter pieces, and ground cinnamon. Use a fork or pastry blender to mix until crumbly and the butter is pea-sized.

8. **Assemble and Bake:**
   - Spread the cake batter evenly into the prepared cake pan.
   - Arrange the sliced apricots on top of the batter in a decorative pattern.
   - Sprinkle the streusel topping evenly over the apricots.
9. **Bake:**
   - Bake in the preheated oven for 30-35 minutes, or until a toothpick inserted into the center comes out clean and the top is golden brown.
10. **Cool and Serve:**
    - Remove the cake from the oven and let it cool in the pan for 10 minutes.
    - Carefully transfer the cake to a wire rack to cool completely before slicing and serving.

Tips:

- Choose ripe but firm apricots for the best texture in the cake.
- If desired, you can sprinkle some sliced almonds or chopped nuts over the streusel topping before baking for added crunch and flavor.
- Serve the Apricot Cake warm or at room temperature. It's delicious on its own or with a dollop of whipped cream or vanilla ice cream.

Enjoy this delicious Apricot Cake, perfect for highlighting the flavors of fresh apricots in a delightful dessert!

Mulberry Cake

Ingredients:

- 2 cups fresh mulberries (washed and stemmed)
- 1 1/2 cups all-purpose flour
- 1 teaspoon baking powder
- 1/4 teaspoon baking soda
- 1/4 teaspoon salt
- 1/2 cup unsalted butter, softened
- 3/4 cup granulated sugar
- 2 large eggs
- 1 teaspoon vanilla extract
- 1/2 cup buttermilk (or regular milk)
- Powdered sugar (for dusting, optional)

Instructions:

1. **Preheat Oven and Prepare Pan:**
    - Preheat your oven to 350°F (175°C). Grease and flour a 9-inch round cake pan or line it with parchment paper.
2. **Prepare Mulberries:**
    - If the mulberries are large, you can cut them in half. Set aside.
3. **Mix Dry Ingredients:**
    - In a bowl, whisk together the flour, baking powder, baking soda, and salt. Set aside.
4. **Cream Butter and Sugar:**
    - In a separate large bowl, cream together the softened butter and granulated sugar until light and fluffy.
5. **Add Eggs and Vanilla:**
    - Beat in the eggs one at a time, then add the vanilla extract and mix until well combined.
6. **Alternate Adding Dry Ingredients and Buttermilk:**
    - Gradually add the dry ingredients to the butter mixture, alternating with the buttermilk. Begin and end with the dry ingredients. Mix until just combined; do not overmix.
7. **Fold in Mulberries:**
    - Gently fold in the fresh mulberries into the batter, being careful not to crush them too much.
8. **Bake:**
    - Pour the batter into the prepared cake pan and spread it evenly. Bake in the preheated oven for 30-35 minutes, or until a toothpick inserted into the center comes out clean.
9. **Cool:**

        - Allow the cake to cool in the pan for about 10 minutes, then remove it from the pan and transfer it to a wire rack to cool completely.
10. **Serve:**
    - Once cooled, dust the top with powdered sugar if desired. Slice and serve your delicious Mulberry Cake!

Enjoy your homemade Mulberry Cake with its delightful burst of berry flavor!